⭐ WEAPONS OF WAR
SUBMARINES
1776–1940

★ WEAPONS OF WAR
SUBMARINES
1776–1940

CHARTWELL BOOKS, INC.

CHARTWELL BOOKS, INC.
A division of BOOK SALES, INC.
276 Fifth Avenue Suite 206
New York, New York 10001
USA

Contributing authors: Chris Chant, Steve Crawford, Martin J. Dougherty, Ian Hogg,
Robert Jackson, Chris McNab, Michael Sharpe, Philip Trewhitt

ISBN 978-0-7858-3001-6

Printed in China

CONTENTS

Introduction

Submarine War

The development of submarines has revolutionized war at sea, making many surface types obselete in the process.

The submarine has revolutionized naval warfare. These vessels, which wage war beneath the waves, have progressed from the crude, steam-driven craft of the American Civil War to silent nuclear submarines that can cruise for months underwater without surfacing, and which carry intercontinental missiles mounting multiple nuclear warheads.

The concept of submarine warfare is centuries old. In 1634, two French priests, Fathers Mersenne and Fornier, produced quite a detailed design for an armed underwater craft, and in 1648, John Wilkins,

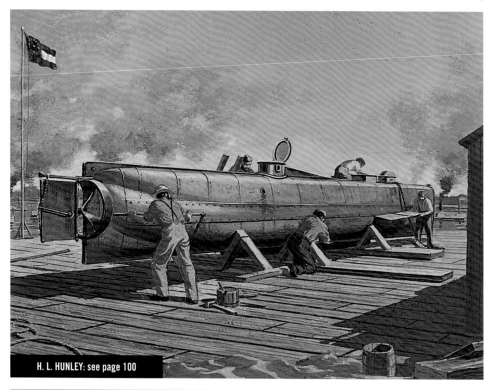

H. L. HUNLEY: see page 100

INTELLIGENT WHALE: see page 111

The *Turtle* was the first submersible to go into action in 1776, against the British in the Hudson River.

Oliver Cromwell's brother-in-law, discussed the possibilities of a 'Submarine Ark'. It was the American War of Independence that saw the first steps in the evolution of the submarine as a true fighting weapon. The first ever underwater mission was undertaken in September 1776, when an American soldier, Ezra Lee, operating a small submersible called *Turtle*, tried to attach an explosive charge to HMS *Eagle* in the Hudson River. Although not a true submersible, all of *Turtle* was under the surface when she was in action except for a tiny conning tower fitted with glass ports so that the sole occupant could find his way to the target. Ezra Lee failed in his mission to attach an explosive charge to the hull of the enemy ship, and the little craft was finally lost when the frigate that was transporting her ran aground.

The Napoleonic Wars might have seen the use of submersible craft in some numbers, had the ideas of an American inventor called Robert Fulton met with success. Having failed to arouse interest with his submarine project in America, Fulton went to France in 1797, where the plans for his prototype submarine were accepted. Launched under the name *Nautilus* in 1800, she was to become the first submarine to be built to a government contract. During trials in Le Havre harbour, *Nautilus* remained

FENIAN RAM: see page 72

WEAPONS OF WAR

HOLLAND VI: see page 106

WEAPONS OF WAR

underwater at a depth of 7.6m (25ft) for one hour. After the French lost interest in the project, Fulton took his design to Britain, where he persuaded Prime Minister William Pitt to examine the idea, but she was not adopted. The attitude of the British Admiralty to the concept was summed up by Lord St Vincent, who denounced Pitt as, 'the greatest fool that ever existed to encourage a mode of warfare which those who commanded the sea did not want, and which, if successful, would deprive them of it.'

In the long peace that followed the defeat of Napoleon there was little incentive for inventive minds to pursue the development of submarine craft, and it took the onset of the American Civil War to create a fresh upsurge of interest. The designs that emerged, however, were little more than suicide craft, armed with an explosive charge on the end of a long pole – the so-called 'spar torpedo'. *H. L. Hunley*, named after her inventor was the first true submersible craft to be used successfully against an enemy. On 17 February 1864, she sank the Union ship *Housatonic*, but was dragged down with her by the wave created by her spar torpedo. Years later, the wreck was located on the sea bed, the skeletons of eight of her crew still seated at their crankshaft.

AMERICAN LEAD

It was the Americans who took the lead in submarine design and development as the turn of the century drew near, and at the forefront was an Irish-American called John P. Holland. Holland's first successful submarine design was his No 1; the diminutive craft was originally designed to be hand-cranked like previous submarines, but with the introduction of the newly developed Brayton four-horsepower petrol engine, Holland was able to produce a more reliable vessel. *Holland No 1* was built at the Albany Iron Works and was completed in 1878. She is now housed in the Paterson Museum, USA. Holland's far-sighted faith in the petrol engine proved premature, other submarine designs of this period being still dependent on steam for their motive power.

The first American submarine of what might be called 'modern' design was *Holland VI*, which later became the prototype for British and Japanese submarines, combining petrol engines and battery power with hydroplanes. *Holland VI* entered service with the US Navy as the Holland in 1900. Although the American press praised the little Holland submarine and bestowed such lurid descriptions as 'Monster War Fish' on her, she was in fact a very primitive craft.

Admiral Sir Arthur Wilson's irascible speech in 1899 denouncing submarines as, 'underhand, unfair and damned un-English' has often been quoted to suggest that the Admiralty had closed its mind on the subject of submarines. The Royal Navy had been alarmed by the sudden proliferation of submarines in the French and American fleets, and in fact an internal study was already underway. The 1901–2 Naval Estimates made provision for the building of five improved boats of the Holland type (an American design) for evaluation. The first five boats to be commissioned were built under licence by Vickers at Barrow-in-Furness; the company and the Navy's newly appointed Inspecting-Captain of Submarines, Captain Reginald Bacon, set

M1: see page 121

WEAPONS OF WAR

L CLASS: see page 118

The first European submarines were designed primarily for operations in the North Sea.

about making a series of improvements, so that when HMS *No 1* was launched on 2 November 1902, she bore little resemblance to her American progenitor. In March 1904, all five boats of the A class, as they were now called, took part in a simulated attack on the cruiser *Juno* off Portsmouth. It was successful, but *A1* was involved in a collision with a passenger liner and sank with the loss of all hands. In all, 13 A class boats were built, followed by 11 B class and 38 C class. From now on, the submarine was to be one of the Royal Navy's principal weapons of war.

TWENTIETH CENTURY DEVELOPMENTS

During the 1900s, some important developments took place. The United Kingdom decided it had to have submarines and its first five were built to Holland's

design. Home-designed B, C, and D classes followed, each one larger than its predecessor. The German Navy, though sceptical, began to build submarines from 1906 and took a lead in using heavy oil rather than vaporous and flammable gasoline, or cumbrous steam machinery, for surface travel. From 1907, the Germans and the British were both building 'overseas' submarines intended primarily for operations in the North Sea, and between 1908 and 1914 the Germans ordered 42 of these, of which 29 were available for service in

August 1914. Boats of this type displaced around 508 tonnes (500 tons) and with the D class (1906) the British too began to use paired diesel engines and twin propellers.

Up to the start of the war, the biggest submarine fleet was the French. The French Navy saw its submarines as compensating for its lack of large capital ships, and naval exercises from the days of *Gustave Zédé* onwards convinced them that the submarine had a role as a potential destroyer of surface warships. By 1906, submarine flotillas were established at Dunkirk, Cherbourg, Rochefort

U47: see page 157

E11: see page 57

By the beginning of World War I, the British, Americans, Russians and French all had substantial submarine fleets.

and Toulon – all important naval ports – with the purpose of operating defensively against any approaching hostile fleet. The French were also the first to send submarines to remote colonial bases, for the same purpose. This French perception of the submarine's role was influential and in other navies it was also seen essentially as a defensive craft. Britain followed the French example by establishing flotilla bases at Devonport, Portsmouth, Harwich and Dundee, to

maintain a watch in the western approaches, the English Channel and the North Sea.

WORLD WAR I

By 1914, the Americans, British, French, Italians and Russians all had substantial submarine fleets. The Germans were slow at first to catch up, but as World War I progressed the German Navy's submarine service became increasingly competent and its boats technologically more advanced,

U32: see page 156

The German U-boats' success in World War I was not forgotten by Nazi Germany's naval planners.

until by the end of 1916 it had become the navy's main offensive arm. Germany's large, long-range 'cruiser' U-boats were a revelation to the Allies, and very nearly brought them to their knees. In 1917 the threat to British merchant ships – which all sailed independently – from U-boats was dire, and in April that year they sank 907,000 tonnes (893,000 tons) of shipping, of which 564,019 tonnes (555,110 tons) were British vessels. It was only the belated introduction of the convoy system that turned things round for the Allies.

The British developed other countermeasures. They built the so-called Dover Barrage, consisting of heavily-armed ships moored in lines across the Channel with minefields, nets and other obstacles between them. However, the vast expenditure of time, labour and materials that the Barrage involved yielded few fruits, with only four U-boats being sunk by the end of 1917. During 1918, (by which time the U-boats had already been defeated in the Atlantic by the convoy system), the barrage did claim between 14 and 26 submarines.

WORLD WAR II: THE BATTLE FOR THE OCEANS

The early successes of the German Navy's U-boat arm were not forgotten in the inter-war years by Nazi Germany's naval planners. The ocean-going U-boat was to prove a fearsome weapon in World War II, and one that came close to bringing Britain to her knees in the bitter conflict known as the Battle of the Atlantic. Admiral Karl Dönitz developed the 'wolf-pack' tactic in an attempt to counter the effectiveness of the convoy system which had defeated him 20 years before. Despite the technical excellence of their boats and the skill and courage of their crews, the Germans lost that battle because the Allies, in particular the British, gradually gave air cover to their convoys, fear of which forced the U-boats to dive; they were thus incapable of keeping up with their targets at their slower submerged speeds.

The majority of U-boats that fought the battle of the Atlantic were Type VIIs. Like the Type II, the Type VII was based on a boat originally designed for Finland and built in 1930. Type VIIs were built in huge numbers, with more than 800 being completed by the end of the war. Although intended for ocean operations, size was limited to allow the maximum number of boats to be built within treaty limits. This had the added advantage of making them agile and quick to dive.

As with most submarines of the period, the Type VII was powered by diesel engines on the surface and used battery-driven electric motors underwater. Under diesel drive it could make more than 17 knots, enough to run rings around a convoy. Underwater it could not do much more than 5 knots, and that for only a few hours.

SURCOUF: see page 145

RUBIS: see page 141

By the middle of World War II, Nazi Germany had developed types of U-boats capable of operating in the Indian Ocean.

The Type VII carried between 11 and 14 torpedoes. Early boats also had a deck gun, but as the war progressed, this was often replaced with a heavy anti-aircraft armament.

The Type IX class was designed for ocean warfare. Loosely based on the far smaller Type II, it differed fundamentally in having a double hull. This increased useable internal volume by enabling fuel and ballast tanks

to be sited externally. In turn, the extra hull improved survivability by cushioning the inner (pressure) hull from explosive shock and gave the boats greatly improved handling on the surface.

Early Type IXs had enough range to operate in the southern hemisphere, mounting long patrols into the waters of the South Atlantic. Later versions with an even greater range could reach the Indian

U106: see page 158

Ocean and even the Pacific without stopping to refuel.

Long-range maritime patrol aircraft, equipped with new detection radar, enjoyed increasing success in locating and destroying the U-boats around their convoys. The same aircraft co-operated on a magnificent scale with Royal Navy and US Navy hunter-killer groups, composed of fast destroyers and frigates that combed the ocean for submarines in a highly-organized pattern and hounded them to destruction in the last two years of the war.

The final cost to the German Navy's U-boat Service was appalling. Of the 1162 U-boats built and commissioned during the war, 785 were recorded as 'spurlos versenkt' (lost without trace). Of the 40,000 officers and men who served in U-boats from 1939 to 1945, 30,000 never returned. Yet there was no escaping the fact that the U-boats, in those years of war, had sunk 2828 Allied merchant ships totalling 14,923,052 tonnes (14,687,321 tons). British naval casualties alone were 80,000, of which more than 30,000 were merchant seamen.

A1

The A-class vessels were the first submarines designed in Britain, although they were originally based on the earlier US Holland type which had entered Royal Navy service in 1901. *A1* was basically a slightly lengthened Holland, but from *A2* onwards they were much larger. They were also the first submarines to be made with a proper conning tower to allow surface running in heavy seas. Originally fitted with a single bow-mounted torpedo tube, the class was equipped with a second tube from *A5* onwards. Built by Vickers, the class helped the Royal Navy to develop and refine its submarine doctrine and operating skills. Thirteen boats were built between 1902 and 1905, and some served in a training capacity during World War I. One of the class (*A7*) was lost with all hands when she dived into the sands at Whitesand Bay.

SPECIFICATIONS

COUNTRY: United Kingdom
LAUNCH DATE: July 1902
CREW: 11
DISPLACEMENT: surfaced 194 tonnes (191 tons); submerged 274.5 tonnes (270 tons)
DIMENSIONS: 30.5m x 3.5m (100ft 1in x 10ft 2in)
ARMAMENT: two 460mm (18in) torpedo tubes
POWERPLANT: one 160hp petrol engine, one 126hp electric motor
RANGE: 593km (320nm) at 10 knots
PERFORMANCE: surfaced 9.5 knots; submerged: 6 knots

Aradam

Aradam was one of the Adua class of 17 short-range vessels. These had a double hull with blisters and were a repeat of the previous Perla class. They gave good service during World War II, and, although their surface speed was low, they were strong and very manoeuvrable. The early boats of the class took part in the Spanish Civil War and all except one (the *Macalle*, which was in the Red Sea) operated in the Mediterranean. Only *Alagi* survived World War II. *Aradam* was scuttled in September 1943 in Genoa harbour to avoid capture by the Germans, who later raised her. She was sunk by Allied bombing in the following year. The class leader, *Adua*, was depth-charged and sunk by the destroyers *Gurkha* and *Legion* on 30 September 1941. Three other units of this class, the original *Ascianghi*, *Gandar* and *Neghelli*, were sold to Brazil prior to launching.

SPECIFICATIONS

COUNTRY: Italy
LAUNCH DATE: 15 November 1936
CREW: 45
DISPLACEMENT: surfaced 691 tonnes (680 tons); submerged 880 tonnes (866 tons)
DIMENSIONS: 60.2m x 6.5m x 4.6m (197ft 6in x 21ft 4in x 15ft 1in)
ARMAMENT: six 530mm (21in) torpedo tubes, one 100mm (3.9in) gun
POWERPLANT: two diesel engines, two electric motors
RANGE: 4076km (2200nm) at 10 knots
PERFORMANCE: surfaced 14 knots; submerged 7 knots

Archimede

The Italian Navy operated five submarines in the Brin class, all completed in 1938–39. The last two, *Archimede* and *Torricelli*, were built in secret to replace two submarines of the same name that had been transferred to the Nationalist forces during the Spanish Civil War. The Brin class were efficient, streamlined vessels, and had a very long range. They had a partial double hull, with four torpedo tubes in the bow and four in the stern. As first completed, the submarines had two 100mm (3.9in) guns. At the outbreak of World War II, *Archimede*

was operating in the Red Sea and the Indian Ocean, where she remained until May 1941. She then made an epic journey round the Cape of Good Hope to Bordeaux, from where she began operations in the Atlantic. She was sunk by Allied aircraft off the coast of Brazil on 14 April 1943.

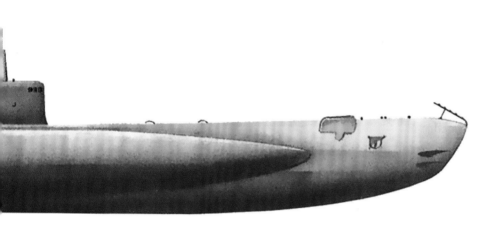

SPECIFICATIONS

COUNTRY: Italy
LAUNCH DATE: 5 March 1939
CREW: 58
DISPLACEMENT: surfaced 1032 tonnes (1016 tons); submerged 1286 tonnes (1266 tons)
DIMENSIONS: 72.4m x 6.7m x 4.5m (237ft 6in x 22ft x 14ft 9in)

ARMAMENT: eight 533mm (21in) torpedo tubes, one 100mm (3.9in) gun
POWERPLANT: two diesels, two electric motors
RANGE: 18,530km (10,000nm) at 10 knots
PERFORMANCE: surfaced 17 knots; submerged: 8 knots

Argonaut (1897)

*A*rgonaut was built by Simon Lake at his own expense as a salvage vessel for inshore waters. A 22kW (30hp) gasoline engine drove the single screw, and the engine could be connected to the twin front wheels for movement along the sea bed; a third wheel aft steered the craft. There was an air chamber forward so that divers could enter and leave. The vessel was rebuilt in 1899 and once made a trip of 3200km (1725nm) on the surface. Successful trials led to a number of export orders, but by that time Lake had lost the initiative to John Holland in the eyes of the US Navy, whose senior officers were not impressed by the idea of a wooden-hulled craft trundling along the sea bed. But the idea was to be resurrected nearly a century later, when designs for 'ocean crawling' submarines were again proposed.

SPECIFICATIONS
COUNTRY: United States
LAUNCH DATE: 1897
CREW: 5
DISPLACEMENT: surfaced not known; submerged 60 tons (59 tons)
DIMENSIONS: 11m x 2.7m (36ft 1in x 8ft 10in)
ARMAMENT: none
POWERPLANT: gasoline engine
RANGE: not known
PERFORMANCE: surfaced 5 knots; submerged 5 knots

Argonaut (1927)

Argonaut was the only purpose-built minelaying submarine to serve in the US Navy. Her pre-war pendant number was *A1*; she was later designated *SS166*. Apart from *Argonaut*, the only minelayers in the US Navy's inventory in 1941 were two old converted coastal passenger ships. On 1 December 1941, with the threat of war with Japan looming, she was stationed with another submarine, USS *Trout*, off Midway for reconnaissance purposes. Shortly after the attack on Pearl Harbor, *Argonaut* was converted to the transport and special duties role, and on 17 August 1942, together with the USS *Nautilus*, she landed the 2nd Raider Battalion in Makin, in the Gilbert Islands, and extracted the force after it had attacked enemy installations. On 10 January 1943, *Argonaut* failed to return from a special operation off Lae.

SPECIFICATIONS

COUNTRY: United States
LAUNCH DATE: 10 November 1927
CREW: 89
DISPLACEMENT: surfaced 2753 tonnes (2710 tons); submerged 4145 tonnes (4080 tons)
DIMENSIONS: 116m x 10.4m x 4.6m (380ft 7in x 34ft 1in x 15ft 6in)
ARMAMENT: four 533mm (21in) torpedo tubes, two 152mm (6in) guns, 60 mines
POWERPLANT: two-shaft diesels, electric motors
RANGE: 10,747km (5800nm) at 10 knots
PERFORMANCE: surfaced 15 knots; submerged 8 knots

Argonaute

Argonaute was the lead boat of five Schneider-Laubeuf submarines, the others being *Aréthuse*, *Atalante*, *La Vestale* and *La Sultane*. All were completed between 1932 and 1935. At the time of the Franco-German Armistice of June 1940, *Argonaute* was in Oran, where she became part of the Vichy French Navy; she was still there in November 1942, when Allied forces invaded North Africa (Operation *Torch*). In places, the French put up considerable resistance to the landings, and a number of naval vessels, including the submarines *Argonaute* and *Actéon*, put to sea to attack the Allied invasion fleet. Both were sunk by the British warships *Achates* and *Westcott*. Another submarine of the class, *La Sultane*, by then serving with the Allies, attacked and probably sank an enemy patrol boat in the Mediterranean on 8 May 1944.

SPECIFICATIONS

COUNTRY: France
LAUNCH DATE: 23 May 1929
CREW: 41
DISPLACEMENT: surfaced 640 tonnes (630 tons); submerged 811 tonnes (798 tons)
DIMENSIONS: 63.4m x 5.2m x 3.61m (208ft 11in x 17ft 1in x 11ft 9in)
ARMAMENT: six 550mm (21.7in) torpedo tubes; one 75mm (3in) gun
POWERPLANT: two diesels, two electric motors
RANGE: 4262km (2300nm) at 7.5 knots
PERFORMANCE: surfaced 13.5 knots; submerged 7.5 knots

Atropo

The Italians placed much faith in mines as offensive weapons, and *Atropo* was one of three Foca-class minelaying submarines built for the Italian Navy just before World War II. As first completed, their 100mm (3.9in) gun was mounted in a training turret, in the after part of the conning tower. This gun was later removed and mounted in the traditional deck position, forward of the conning tower. The class leader, *Foca*, was lost on 15 October 1940 while laying a mine barrage off Haifa; the general opinion was that she had run into a British minefield. *Atropo* and the third vessel, *Zoea*, survived the war and were discarded in 1947. Late in 1943, now on the Allied side, *Atropo* joined other Italian submarines in running supplies to British garrisons on the Aegean islands of Samos and Leros.

SPECIFICATIONS

COUNTRY: Italy
LAUNCH DATE: 20 November 1938
CREW: 60
DISPLACEMENT: surfaced 234.6 tonnes (231 tons); submerged 325 tonnes (320 tons)
DIMENSIONS: 44.5m x 4.4m x 2.7m (146ft x 14ft 5in x 8ft 10in)
ARMAMENT: two 450mm (17.7in) torpedo tubes, one 100mm (3.9in) gun, 36 mines
POWERPLANT: two diesels, two electric motors
RANGE: 11,118km (6000nm) at 10 knots
PERFORMANCE: surfaced 15.2 knots; submerged 7.4 knots

B1

Construction of the improved B-class submarines was under way before the A-class boats were completed. An extended superstructure on top of the hull gave improved surface performance, while small hydroplanes on the conning tower improved underwater handling. By 1910 the Royal Navy had 11 B-class boats. They were not comfortable craft in which to serve; their interior stank of raw fuel, bilge-water and dampness, all pervaded by a stench of oil, and when submerged there was a constant risk of explosion from violent sparks produced by unshieded electrical components in an atmosphere saturated with petrol vapour. Six B-class submarines were sent to Gibraltar and Malta. *B1* was broken up in 1921. The first RN VC of World War I was awarded to a B-class boat commander.

SPECIFICATIONS

COUNTRY: Britain
LAUNCH DATE: October 1904
CREW: 16
DISPLACEMENT: surfaced 284 tonnes (280 tons); submerged 319 tonnes (314 tons)
DIMENSIONS: 41m x 4.1m x 3m (134ft 6in x 13ft 6in x 9ft 10in)
ARMAMENT: two 475mm (18in) torpedo tubes
POWERPLANT: single screw petrol engine, electric motor
RANGE: 2779km (1500nm) at 8 knots
PERFORMANCE: surfaced 13 knots; submerged 7 knots

Balilla

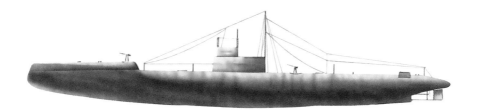

Balilla was originally ordered by the Germany Navy from an Italian yard and was allocated the number *U42*, but the boat never saw German service. Taken over by the Italian Navy in 1915 and named *Balilla*, she saw some service in the Adriatic, but while on patrol on 14 July 1916 she was sunk by Austrian torpedo boats with the loss of all 38 crew members. The principal task of the Italian submarines operating in the Adriatic in World War I was to patrol the coastline of Dalmatia, which had many harbours and inlets that were used by the Austro-Hungarian fleet. Operating conditions were difficult, as the waters were fairly shallow and it was not easy to take evasive action if attacked. Both Austrians and Italians made extensive use of seaplanes once it was found that submerged submarines could often be seen from them.

SPECIFICATIONS

COUNTRY: Italy
LAUNCH DATE: August 1913
CREW: 38
DISPLACEMENT: surfaced 740 tonnes (728 tons); submerged 890 tonnes (876 tons)
DIMENSIONS: 65m x 6m x 4m (213ft 3in x 19ft 8in x 13ft 1in)
ARMAMENT: four 450mm (17.7in) torpedo tubes, two 76mm (3in) guns
POWERPLANT: two-shaft diesel/electric motors
RANGE: 7041km (3800nm) at 10 knots
PERFORMANCE: surfaced 14 knots; submerged 9 knots

Barbarigo (1917)

The first *Barbarigo* was one of a group of four medium-sized submarines laid down in October 1915, but not completed until the end of World War I. The batteries were placed in four watertight compartments under the horizontal deck that ran the full length of the vessel. This was a new arrangement, as the batteries were usually concentrated in one large compartment for ease of access, and was designed as a safety measure to prevent the release of chlorine gas in large quantities in the event of seawater infiltrating into the boat and making accidental contact with the batteries. The Barbarigo class had a range of just over 3218km (1734nm) at 11 knots, but their maximum diving depth was only 50m (164ft). The Italians never managed to exploit their submarines to the full. *Barbarigo* was sold in 1928.

SPECIFICATIONS

COUNTRY: Italy
LAUNCH DATE: November 1917
CREW: 35
DISPLACEMENT: surfaced 774 tonnes (762 tons); submerged 938 tonnes (923 tons)
DIMENSIONS: 67m x 6m x 3.8m (219ft 10in x 19ft 8in x 12ft 6in)
ARMAMENT: six 450mm (17.7in) torpedo tubes, two 76mm (3in) guns
POWERPLANT: twin shaft diesel/electric motors
RANGE: 3218km (1734nm) at 11 knots
PERFORMANCE: surfaced 16 knots; submerged 9.8 knots

Barbarigo (1938)

Barbarigo was one of a class of nine units, only one of which survived World War II. These vessels were built with a partial double hull and internal ballast tanks. They were reasonably fast and manoeuvrable, but had poor transverse stability. This characteristic was aggravated by the long conning tower, a common feature of Italian submarines during this period. The class also had a relatively short range, some 1425km (768nm) on the surface and 228km (123nm) submerged at three knots. Maximum diving depth was about 100m (328ft). *Barbarigo* was completed in 1939 and, after more than four years of active service, she was converted into a transport submarine to ferry supplies to Japan. Her first such voyage was in June 1943, but she was sighted by Allied aircraft on the surface in the Bay of Biscay, attacked and sunk.

SPECIFICATIONS
COUNTRY: Italy
LAUNCH DATE: 13 June 1938
CREW: 58
DISPLACEMENT: surfaced 1059 tonnes (1043 tons); submerged 1310 tonnes (1290 tons)
DIMENSIONS: 73m x 7m x 5m (239ft 6in x 23ft x 16ft 6in)
ARMAMENT: eight 533mm (21in) torpedo tubes
POWERPLANT: twin shaft diesel/electric motors
RANGE: 1425km (768nm) at 10 knots
PERFORMANCE: surfaced 17.4 knots; submerged 8 knots

Bass

The USS *Bass* was one of three submarines of the Barracuda class, built at the Portsmouth Navy Yard in the mid-1920s. The first post-World War I submarines, these fast fleet boats were the first of nine authorized as part of the major 1916 programme. They were about twice the size of the earlier S-class boats, and were even bigger than the three wartime T-class craft broken up under the terms of the 1930 London Treaty. The boats were partly re-engined before World War II. Their war service was limited to training, and plans to convert them to transport submarines were abandoned although they might have proved very useful in this role. On 17 August 1942, *Bass* lost half her crew when a serious fire broke out in the engine room while she was at sea. She was scuttled on 14 July 1945.

SPECIFICATIONS

COUNTRY: United States
LAUNCH DATE: 27 December 1924
CREW: 85
DISPLACEMENT: surfaced 2032 tonnes (2000 tons); submerged 2662 tonnes (2620 tons)
DIMENSIONS: 99.4m x 8.3m x 4.5m (326ft 1in x 27ft 3in x 14ft 9in)
ARMAMENT: six 533mm (21in) torpedo tubes; one 76mm (3in) gun
POWERPLANT: two-shaft diesel engines, electric motors
RANGE: 11,118km (6000nm) at 11 knots
PERFORMANCE: surfaced 18 knots; submerged 11 knots

Beta

In 1912, two small experimental submarines were built in the Venice Naval Yard for harbour surveillance and defence. They did not serve in the Italian Navy, but were given the temporary names of *Alfa* and *Beta*. Next came the 31.4-tonne (31-ton) A class of 1915-16, closely followed by the B class of which *Beta* was part. She was better known as the *B1*. Only three of the class became operative – as harbour defence vessels – with three more being broken up in 1920 before completion. Harbour defence on Italy's Adriatic coast posed few problems, as virtually the only harbour of any consequence in World War I was Trieste; the Austrians, on the other hand, made use of many harbours and anchorages, and their defences were badly overstretched. Few of the naval actions in the Adriatic had a conclusive result.

SPECIFICATIONS

COUNTRY: Italy
LAUNCH DATE: July 1916
CREW: 20
DISPLACEMENT: surfaced 40 tonnes (39 tons); submerged 46 tonnes (45 tons)
DIMENSIONS: 15m x 2.3m x 2.5m (49ft 7in x 7ft 8in x 8ft 3in)
ARMAMENT: two 450mm (17.7in) torpedo tubes
POWERPLANT: single screw petrol engine, electric motor
RANGE: not known
PERFORMANCE: surfaced 8 knots; submerged not known

Blaison

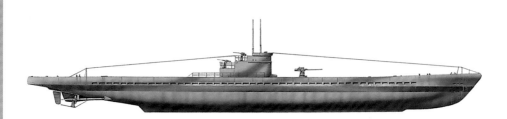

Blaison was formerly the German Type IXB submarine *U-123*. She was operational from May 1940 until August 1944, when – unable for technical reasons to comply with orders to break out of Lorient and sail for Norway – she was scuttled. She was raised and commissioned into the French Navy as *Blaison* in 1947, serving until 1951. She was then placed in reserve and eventually scrapped in August 1958. Several other ex-German submarines also served with the French Navy post-war; they were the Type IXC U510, which surrendered at St Nazaire and became the *Bouan*; the Type VIIC U471, which was repared after being damaged by air attack at Toulon and commissioned as *Mille*; and the Type VIIC U766, which surrendered at La Pallice and became the *Laubie*. The most sought-after prize, though, was the new Type XXI.

SPECIFICATIONS

COUNTRY: France
LAUNCH DATE: May 1940
CREW: 48
DISPLACEMENT: surfaced 1050 tonnes (1034 tons); submerged 1178 tonnes (1159 tons)
DIMENSIONS: 76.5m x 6.8m x 4.7m (251ft x 22ft 4in x 15ft 5in)
ARMAMENT: six 533mm (21in) torpedo tubes; one 105mm (4.1in) gun
POWERPLANT: two twin-shaft diesel engines, two electric motors
RANGE: 4632km (2500nm) at 16 knots
PERFORMANCE: surfaced 18 knots; submerged 7.3 knots

Brin

Brin (named after the celebrated Italian naval engineer Benedetto Brin) was one of a class of long-range submarines with a partial double hull developed from the Archimede class. A distinguishing feature of the Brin class was their tall conning tower. She was active from the beginning of Italy's involvement in World War II, initially forming part of a submarine squadron covering the approaches to the Aegean Sea. In 1941, as part of an Italian submarine group based on French Atlantic ports, *Brin* operated against Allied convoys in the sea area west of Gibraltar. Following the Italian armistice in September 1943, *Brin*, under Allied command, transferred to Ceylon and was used to train Allied anti-submarine warfare forces in the Indian Ocean, a role in which she became quite famous. She was discarded in 1948.

SPECIFICATIONS

COUNTRY: Italy
LAUNCH DATE: 03 April 1938
CREW: 58
DISPLACEMENT: surfaced 1032 tonnes (1016 tons); submerged 1286 tonnes (1266 tons)
DIMENSIONS: 70m x 7m x 4.2m (231ft 4in x 22ft 6in x 13ft 6in)
ARMAMENT: eight 533mm (21in) torpedo tubes, one 100mm (3.9in) gun
POWERPLANT: twin-screw diesel engines, two electric motors
RANGE: 18,530km (10,000nm) at 10 knots
PERFORMANCE: surfaced 17 knots; submerged 8 knots

C1 class

The C1 class of submarine, designated I-16 in Japanese Navy service, was the product of a massive naval building programme initiated by the Japanese government after the expiry of the London Naval Treaty. There were five boats in the class (*I-16*, *I-18*, *I-20*, *I-22* and *I-24*) and they had an extremely long radius of action, being able to remain at sea for 90 days without replenishment. At the beginning of 1943, *I-16* had her 140mm (5.5in) gun removed and the number of torpedoes reduced. With special fittings she could carry a 14m (46ft) landing craft, or equipment and stores for Japanese troops on islands isolated by the Allied advance. The *I-16* was sunk off the Solomon Islands by a 'hedgehog' ASW mortar salvo from a US destroyer escort group on 19 May 1944. The USS *England* of this group sank six Japanese submarines in 12 days.

SPECIFICATIONS

COUNTRY: Japan
LAUNCH DATE: 28 July 1938
CREW: 100
DISPLACEMENT: surfaced 2605 tonnes (2564 tons); submerged 3761 tonnes (3701 tons)
DIMENSIONS: 108.6m x 9m x 5m (256ft 3in x 29ft 5in x 16ft 4in)
ARMAMENT: eight 533mm (21in) torpedo tubes; one 140mm (5.5in) gun
POWERPLANT: two-shaft diesel/electric motors
RANGE: 25,928km (14,000nm)
PERFORMANCE: surfaced 23.5 knots; submerged 8 knots

C3

All the C-class boats gave good service to the Royal Navy, and were well-liked by their crews. In 1910 – by which time 37 were in service – three of them, escorted by the sloop *Rosario*, were towed to the Far East to join the China Squadron at Hong Kong, a truly epic voyage for submarines in those early pioneer days, and three more went to Gibraltar. During World War I, four C-class boats were sent to Russia, but were scuttled to prevent them falling into German hands in the Baltic. *C3* herself had a dramatic exit; on 23 April 1918 she was filled with high explosive and, commanded by Lt Richard D. Sandford, crept into Zeebrugge harbour and was exploded under a steel viaduct as part of the British blocking operation there. The two officers and four men aboard were picked up, although wounded; Sandford was awarded the Victoria Cross.

SPECIFICATIONS

COUNTRY: United Kingdom
LAUNCH DATE: 1906
CREW: 16
DISPLACEMENT: surfaced 295 tonnes (290 tons); submerged 325 tonnes (320 tons)
DIMENSIONS: 43m x 4m x 3.5m (141ft 1in x 13ft 1in x 11ft 4in)
ARMAMENT: two 457mm (18in) torpedo tubes
POWERPLANT: single screw petrol engine, one electric motor
RANGE: 2414km (1431nm) at 8 knots
PERFORMANCE: surfaced 12 knots; submerged 7.5 knots

C25

The C class of submarine was the first to be produced in substantial numbers for the Royal Navy. *C25* was part of the second batch of boats (*C19* to *C38*), completed in 1909–10. Despite their limitations, the C boats were active in World War I. Because of their small size, four were shipped to north Russia, broken into sections and transported overland to be reassembled for use in the Gulf of Finland. C boats were sometimes towed submerged by decoy trawlers to counter small U-boats that were harassing Britain's North Sea fishing fleet, a ruse that resulted in the destruction of two of the enemy before the Germans realised what was happening. Four C-class boats were lost in the war, and the four boats in the Gulf of Finland were eventually blown up to prevent their seizure by Communist forces after the White Russian collapse.

SPECIFICATIONS

COUNTRY: United KIngdom
LAUNCH DATE: 1909
CREW: 16
DISPLACEMENT: surfaced 295 tonnes (290 tons); submerged 325 tonnes (320 tons)
DIMENSIONS: 43m x 4m x 3.5m (141ft 1in x 13ft 1in x 11ft 4in)
ARMAMENT: two 457mm (18in) torpedo tubes
POWERPLANT: single screw petrol engine, one electric motor
RANGE: 2414km (1431nm) at 8 knots
PERFORMANCE: surfaced 12 knots; submerged 7.5 knots

Casabianca

Casabianca was one of the last batch of six boats (there were 29 in all, laid down in six batches between 1925 and 1931) of the Redoutable class. They were designated First Class Submarines, but they were dogged by early misfortune when *Promethée* was lost during trials on 8 July 1932 and *Phénix* was lost in unknown circumstances in Indo-Chinese waters on 15 June 1939. Of the remainder, 11 were scuttled either at Toulon or Brest when the Germans occupied the Vichy French zone in November 1942 and others were lost during Allied attacks on Vichy French naval assets in North Africa. *Casabianca* played a proud part in the liberation of Corsica, sinking two German anti-submarine patrol boats in December 1943 and severely damaging an Italian cargo ship. Free French crews handled their boats with great skill and courage.

SPECIFICATIONS

COUNTRY: France
LAUNCH DATE: 2 February 1935
CREW: 61
DISPLACEMENT: surfaced 1595 tonnes (1570 tons); submerged 2117 tonnes (2084 tons)
DIMENSIONS: 92.3m x 8.2m x 4.7m (302ft 10in x 18ft 7in x 10ft 9in)
ARMAMENT: nine 550mm (21.7in) and two 400mm (15.7in) torpedo tubes; one 100mm (3.9in) gun
POWERPLANT: two twin-shaft diesel engines, two electric motors
RANGE: 18,530km (10,000nm) at 10 knots
PERFORMANCE: surfaced 17–20 knots; submerged 10 knots

Corallo

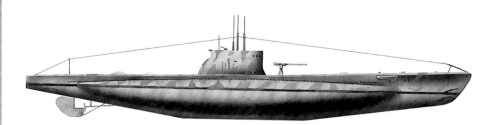

Corallo was one of ten submarines of the Perla class, all completed in 1936. Two of the class, *Iride* and *Onice*, served under the Nationalist flag in the Spanish Civil War, bearing the temporary names *Gonzalez Lopez* and *Aguilar Tablada*. During World War II, *Iride*, together with a sister boat, *Ambra*, were modified to carry human torpedoes. In September 1940, *Corallo* took part in a failed attack on the aircraft carrier HMS *Illustrious* and the battleship HMS *Valiant*. During the next two years, she enjoyed some small success, sinking two sailing vessels off the North African coast, but on 13 December 1942, *Corallo* was sunk off Bougie by the British sloop *Enchantress*, the submarine *Porfido* being sunk in the same action by the British submarine *Tigris*. The British cruiser *Argonaut* was damaged by a torpedo.

SPECIFICATIONS

COUNTRY: Italy
LAUNCH DATE: 02 August 1936
CREW: 45
DISPLACEMENT: surfaced 707 tonnes (696 tons); submerged 865 tonnes (852 tons)
DIMENSIONS: 60m x 6.5m x 5m (196ft 9in x 21ft 2in x 15ft 3in)
ARMAMENT: six 533mm (21in) torpedo tubes, one 100mm (3.9in) gun
POWERPLANT: two diesel engines, two electric motors
RANGE: 6670km (3595nm) at 10 knots
PERFORMANCE: surfaced 14 knots; submerged 8 knots

D1

With the D-class submarines, the British made their first attempt to produce vessels that could be used on extended patrols away from coastal areas. The D class had increased displacement, diesel engines and greater internal space. Unlike earlier classes, the D class could send wireless messages as well as receive them. On the outbreak of World War I in August 1914, the eight D-class boats of the Dover-based 8th Flotilla were assigned to screen the convoys that were ferrying troops of the British Expeditionary Force across the Channel to France and to push out offensive patrols into the Heligoland Bight. The 8th Flotilla at Harwich was commanded by Commodore Roger Keyes, and, as well as the D-class boats, comprised nine E-class submarines. *D1* was sunk as a floating target in 1918.

SPECIFICATIONS

COUNTRY: United Kingdom
LAUNCH DATE: August 1908
CREW: 25
DISPLACEMENT: surfaced 490 tonnes (483 tons); submerged 604 tonnes (595 tons)
DIMENSIONS: 50m x 6m x 3m (164ft 1in x 20ft 6in x 10ft 5in)
ARMAMENT: three 457mm (18in) torpedo tubes, one 12-pounder gun
POWERPLANT: twin-screw diesel engines, electric motors
RANGE: 2038km (1100nm) at 10 knots
PERFORMANCE: surfaced 14 knots; submerged 9 knots

Dagabur

Dagabur was one of the Adua class of 17 boats built for the Italian Navy in the years immediately before the outbreak of World War II. Two of the class – *Gondar* and *Scire* – were modified in 1940–41 for the transport of human torpedoes in three cylinders that were attached to the outside central part of the hull, fore and aft of the conning tower. In December 1941, it was the *Scire* that infiltrated human torpedo crews into Alexandria harbour to make successful attacks on the British battleships *Valiant* and *Queen Elizabeth*. On 12 August 1942, *Dagabur* was part of a strong force despatched to attack the vital 'Pedestal' supply convoy to Malta; she was attempting to set up an attack on the aircraft carrier HMS *Furious* when she was rammed and sunk by the destroyer *Wolverine*.

SPECIFICATIONS

COUNTRY: Italy
LAUNCH DATE: 22 November 1936
CREW: 45
DISPLACEMENT: surfaced 690 tonnes (680 tons); submerged 861 tonnes (848 tons)
DIMENSIONS: 60m x 6.5m x 4m (197ft 6in x 21ft 4in x 13ft 2in)
ARMAMENT: six 533mm (21in) torpedo tubes, one 100mm (3.9in) gun
POWERPLANT: twin-screw diesel engines, electric motors
RANGE: 4076km (2200nm) at 10 knots
PERFORMANCE: surfaced 14 knots; submerged 8 knots

Dandolo

Dandolo, a long-range, single hull boat with internal ballast tanks, was one of the nine vessels of the Marcello class, among the best Italian ocean-going submarines to see service in World War II. In the late summer of 1940, *Dandolo* moved to Bordeaux with other Italian submarines to begin offensive operations in the Central Atlantic, where she sank one ship of 5270 tonnes (5187 tons), and damaged another of 3828 tonnes (3768 tons). She remained at Bordeaux for several months during the winter of 1940–41 – during which time there were actually more Italian submarines than German U-boats operating in the Atlantic area – before returning to the Mediterranean, where she scored further successes, including the torpedoing of the cruiser *Cleopatra* in July 1943. The only boat of her class to survive the war, *Dandalo* was scrapped in 1947.

SPECIFICATIONS

COUNTRY: Italy
LAUNCH DATE: 20 November 1937
CREW: 57
DISPLACEMENT: surfaced 1080 tonnes (1063 tons); submerged 1338 tonnes (1317 tons)
DIMENSIONS: 73m x 7.2m x 5m (239ft 6in x 23ft 8in x 16ft 5in)
ARMAMENT: eight 533mm (21in) torpedo tubes; two 100mm (3.9in) guns
POWERPLANT: twin-screw diesel engines, electric motors
RANGE: 4750km (2560nm) at 17 knots
PERFORMANCE: surfaced 17.4 knots; submerged 8 knots

Delfino (1890)

Constructed at La Spezia Naval Dockyard, *Delfino* was the first submarine built for the Italian Navy. She was rebuilt in 1902 with increased dimensions and displacement. A petrol engine was added and the conning tower enlarged. *Delfino* was discarded in 1918. She was powered originally by only an electric motor, but in 1902 or thereabouts, she was fitted with a petrol engine for use on the surface. Sometimes known as the *Delfino-Pullino*, she may have been laid down in the autumn of 1889 and launched either in 1890 or 1892. The fact is that a good deal of ambiguity is attached to the various key dates in her career. What is fairly certain is that she was completed in 1892 and that she completed her first sea trials in April that year. According to official sources, *Delfino* was commissioned in 1896, but other sources claim that she was commissioned in April 1892.

SPECIFICATIONS

COUNTRY: Italy
LAUNCH DATE: 1890 or 1892
CREW: 8–11
DISPLACEMENT: surfaced 96 tonnes (95 tons); submerged 108 tonnes (107 tons)
DIMENSIONS: 24m x 3m x 2.5m (78ft 9in x 9ft 5in x 8ft 4in)
ARMAMENT: two 355mm (14in) torpedo tubes
POWERPLANT: one petrol engine, one electric motor
RANGE: not known
PERFORMANCE: surfaced not known; submerged not known

Delfino (1931)

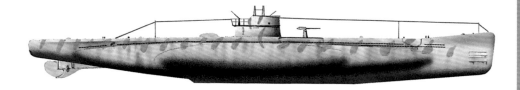

Completed in 1931, *Delfino* was one of the Squalo class of vessels, only one of which survived World War II. The Squalo-class boats were the project of General Engineer Curio Bernardis. During the first months of Italy's war, she operated in the Aegean and off Crete. On 30 July 1941, *Delfino* was attacked by a British Sunderland flying boat off Mersa Matruh, but succeeded in shooting it down and took four survivors prisoner. Apart from that, her operations brought no success. On 23 March 1943, *Delfino* was accidentally sunk off Taranto by a collision with a pilot boat. Of her sister boats, *Narvalo* was scuttled after being damaged by British destroyers off Tripoli in January 1943; *Tricheco* was sunk by HMS *Upholder* off Brindisi in March 1942, and *Squalo* was discarded in 1948.

SPECIFICATIONS

COUNTRY: Italy
LAUNCH DATE: 27 April 1930
CREW: 52
DISPLACEMENT: surfaced 948 tonnes (933 tons); submerged 1160 tonnes (1142 tons)
DIMENSIONS: 70m x 7m x 7m (229ft 8in x 23ft x 23ft)
ARMAMENT: eight 533mm (21in) torpedo tubes, one 102mm (4in) gun
POWERPLANT: two diesel engines, two electric motors
RANGE: 7412km (4000nm) at 10 knots
PERFORMANCE: surfaced 15 knots; submerged 8 knots

Deutschland

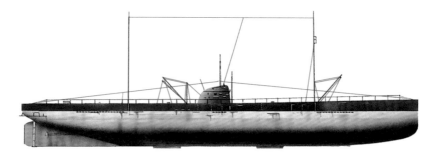

Before America's entry into the war in 1917, the Germans were quick to recognize the potential of large, cargo-carrying submarines as a means of beating the blockade imposed on Germany's ports by the Royal Navy. Two U151-class submarines, the *U151* and *U155*, were converted for mercantile use and named *Oldenburg* and *Deutschland* respectively. Both were unarmed. *Deutschland* made two commercial runs to the United States before America's involvement in the war brought an end to the venture; she was then converted back to naval use, as was *Oldenburg*. *Deutschland* was scrapped at Morecambe, England, in 1922, while *Oldenburg* was sunk as a target off Cherbourg in 1921. A third merchant conversion, *Bremen*, was lost on her first voyage in 1917, possibly mined off the Orkneys.

SPECIFICATIONS

COUNTRY: Germany
LAUNCH DATE: March 1916
CREW: 56
DISPLACEMENT: surfaced 1536 tonnes (1512 tons); submerged 1905 tonnes (1875 tons)
DIMENSIONS: 65m x 8.9m x 5.3m (213ft 3in x 29ft 2in x 17ft 5in)
ARMAMENT: none
POWERPLANT: twin-screw diesel engines, electric motors
RANGE: 20,909km (11,284nm) at 10 knots
PERFORMANCE: surfaced 12.4 knots; submerged 5.2 knots

Diaspro

One of the ten Perla-class submarines that were all involved in the Spanish Civil War before the outbreak of World War II, *Diaspro* had a singularly undistinguished combat career, in common with many other Italian submarines. It is a fact – with few exceptions – that Italian submarine commanders failed to prosecute their operations with vigour and determination, being reluctant to attack Allied naval forces and convoys if the odds against them seemed unfavourable. What they might have achieved was revealed, doubtless to their humiliation, when the Germans stepped up the number of U-boats operating in the Mediterranean, and began to take a dramatic toll of Allied shipping from the Levant to Gibraltar, with little regard for their own danger. *Diaspro* survived the war and was stricken in 1948.

SPECIFICATIONS

COUNTRY: Italy
LAUNCH DATE: 5 July 1936
CREW: 45
DISPLACEMENT: surfaced 711 tonnes (700 tons); submerged 873 tonnes (860 tons)
DIMENSIONS: 60m x 6.4m x 4.6m (197ft 5in x 21ft 2in x 15ft 1in)
ARMAMENT: six 533mm (21in) torpedo tubes; one 100mm (3.9in) gun
POWERPLANT: twin-screw diesel engines, eletric motors
RANGE: 6670km (3595nm) at 10 knots
PERFORMANCE: surfaced 14 knots; submerged 8 knots

Dolphin

During the 1920s, the Americans built a succession of various submarine types, known collectively as the V class. *Dolphin* was an experimental boat, originally designated *V7* and then given the serial number SS169. She was a distinct departure from the large ocean-going boats that were then popular, towards a more modest long-range type. She was not considered a success, however, because of an attempt to incorporate most of the features of the preceding class into a hull half the size. During World War II, *Dolphin* was relegated to training duties. She was broken up in 1946. As a matter of interest, the previous class – the Narwhal boats – were successful. *Narwhal* and *Nautilus* transported the 2nd Raider Battalion to Makin in the Gilbert Islands for an attack on Japanese installations in August 1942.

SPECIFICATIONS

COUNTRY: United States
LAUNCH DATE: 8 March 1932
CREW: 60
DISPLACEMENT: surfaced 1585 tonnes (1560 tons); submerged 2275 tonnes (2240 tons)
DIMENSIONS: 97m x 8.5m x 4m (319ft 3in x 27ft 9in x 13ft 3in)
ARMAMENT: six 533mm (21in) torpedo tubes; one 102mm (4in) gun
POWERPLANT: twin-screw diesel engines, electric motors
RANGE: 11,112km (6000nm) at 10 knots
PERFORMANCE: surfaced 17 knots; submerged 8 knots

Domenico Millelire

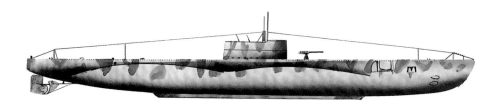

Domenico *Millelire* was one of four boats of the Balilla class which were all built at the Ansaldo-San Giorgio Yards. They were the first large submarines built for the Italian Navy, and they all made numerous long-range ocean cruises in the 1930s. They also participated in the Spanish Civil War on the Nationalist side, bearing false identities. The *Millelire* carried out early war patrols off Crete and convoy protection duty in the Strait of Otranto, at the entrance to the Adriatic. She was laid up on 15 April 1941 and used as a floating oil depot, bearing the registration GR248. The class leader, *Balilla*, was also laid up in the same month and used for similar purposes. A third boat, *Antonio Sciesa*, was scuttled after being damaged in an air attack on Tobruk, while the fourth, *Enrico Toti*, was laid up in April 1943.

SPECIFICATIONS

COUNTRY: Italy
LAUNCH DATE: 19 September 1927
CREW: 76
DISPLACEMENT: surfaced 1585 tonnes (1560 tons); submerged 2275 tonnes (2240 tons)
DIMENSIONS: 97m x 8.5m x 4m (319ft 3in x 27ft 9in x 13ft 1in)
ARMAMENT: six 533mm (21in) torpedo tubes; one 102mm (4in) gun
POWERPLANT: twin-screw diesels, one auxiliary motor, two electric motors
RANGE: 7401km (3800nm) at 10 knots
PERFORMANCE: surfaced 17.5 knots; submerged 8.9 knots

Dupuy de Lôme

Dupuy de Lôme was laid down as part of the 1913 naval construction programme. She served with the Morocco Flotilla from 1917 until the end of World War I, and was then reconstructed. Her steam engines were replaced by diesels taken from German submarines which developed 2163kW (2900hp). Dupuy de Lôme was discarded in 1935. The submarine was named after Stanislas Charles Henri Laurent Dupuy de Lôme (1816–85), the talented naval engineer who designed the first screw-driven warship, Napoléon, and the first French armoured battleship, Gloire. Both the French and Italians had a tendency to name their warships after engineers and statesmen, a practice not adopted by the Royal Navy. The previous warship to carry the name was a cruiser, launched in 1890 and sold to Peru in 1912.

SPECIFICATIONS

COUNTRY: France
LAUNCH DATE: September 1915
CREW: 54
DISPLACEMENT: surfaced 846 tonnes (833 tons); submerged 1307 tonnes (1287 tons)
DIMENSIONS: 75m x 6.4m x 3.6m (246ft 1in x 21ft x 11ft 10in)
ARMAMENT: eight 450mm (17.7in) torpedo tubes
POWERPLANT: twin-screw 3-cylinder reciprocating steam engine; electric motors
RANGE: 10,469km (5650nm) at 10 knots
PERFORMANCE: surfaced 15 knots; submerged 8.5 knots

Durbo

Durbo was one of the 17-strong Adua class of submarines, built in the years immediately before World War II. The Adua class might well be called the workhorses of Italy's wartime submarine fleet. Italy's entry into the conflict in June 1940 found *Durbo* at her war station in the Sicilian Channel; in July she moved to a new station off Malta, and early in September, together with two other submarines, she failed to locate and intercept a supply convoy that was approaching the island. *Durbo's* end came on 18 October 1940 when she was operating to the east of Gibraltar; located by two SARO London flying boats of No 202 Squadron RAF, she was attacked and sunk by the destroyers *Firedrake* and *Wrestler*. Another Adua-class submarine operating in the area, *Lafole*, was sunk on 20 October by the destroyers *Gallant*, *Griffin* and *Hotspur*.

SPECIFICATIONS

COUNTRY: Italy
LAUNCH DATE: 6 March 1938
CREW: 45
DISPLACEMENT: surfaced 710 tonnes (698 tons); submerged 880 tonnes (866 tons)
DIMENSIONS: 60m x 6.4m x 4m (197ft 6in x 21ft x 13ft 2in)
ARMAMENT: six 533mm (21in) torpedo tubes; one 100mm (3.9in) gun
POWERPLANT: twin-screw diesel engines, electric motors
RANGE: 4076km (2200nm) at 10 knots
PERFORMANCE: surfaced 14 knots; submerged 7.5 knots

Dykkeren

Dykkeren was built in Italy by Fiat-San Giorgio, La Spezia. She was sold to the Danish Navy in October 1909. She had many teething troubles, but improved at the Copenhagen Naval Yard. In 1916, she was in collision with the Norwegian steamer Vesta off Bergen, and sank. Salvaged in 1917, Dykkeren was broken up the following year. Although a small country, Denmark maintained a strong and efficient navy for coastal defence, and in fact possessed one of the world's first ironclads (the Rolf Krake). A number of ironclad warships were built for coastal defence and two were purchased which had been intended for the Confederate Navy. Denmark succeeded in maintaining its neutrality throughout the various European conflicts until 1940, when the country was occupied by German forces. She acquired four patrol submarines post-World War II.

SPECIFICATIONS

COUNTRY: Denmark
LAUNCH DATE: June 1909
CREW: 35
DISPLACEMENT: surfaced 107 tonnes (105 tons); submerged 134 tonnes (132 tons)
DIMENSIONS: 34.7m x 3.3m x 2m (113ft 10in x 10ft 10in x 6ft 6in)
ARMAMENT: two 457mm (18in) torpedo tubes
POWERPLANT: twin-screw petrol engine, one electric motor
RANGE: 185km (100nm) at 12 knots
PERFORMANCE: surfaced 12 knots; submerged 7.5 knots

E11

Completed between 1913 and 1916, the E-class submarines ran to 55 hulls whose construction, once war was declared, was shared between 13 private yards. They fell into five major groups, differences being primarily in torpedo layout and the adaptation of six boats to carry 20 mines in place of their amidships tubes. *E11*, under the command of the talented Lt Cdr Martin Nasmith, was arguably the most famous of them all; operating in the Dardanelles area she scored many successes, including the sinking of the Turkish battleship *Hairredin Barbarossa*. Many RN submariners who rose to high rank learned their trade in E-class boats. For operations in the Dardanelles, the British submarines adopted a blue camouflage to conceal themselves in the shallow, clear waters. The class was also active in the North Sea and the Baltic. In all, 22 were lost.

SPECIFICATIONS

COUNTRY: United KIngdom
LAUNCH DATE: 1913
CREW: 30
DISPLACEMENT: surfaced 677 tonnes (667 tons); submerged 820 tonnes (807 tons)
DIMENSIONS: 55.17m x 6.91m x 3.81m (181ft x 22ft 8in x 12ft 6in)
ARMAMENT: five 457mm (18in) torpedo tubes; one 12-pounder gun
POWERPLANT: two twin-shaft diesel engines, two electric motors
RANGE: 6035km (3579nm)
PERFORMANCE: surfaced 14 knots; submerged 9 knots

E20

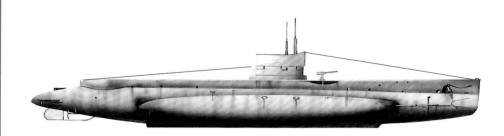

The excellent combat radius of the E-class boats enabled them to mount extended patrols in enemy waters from relatively distant bases. *E20*'s hunting ground was the Sea of Marmara, where she was sunk on 5 November 1915 by the German submarine *UB14*; this was the first instance of a submarine sinking another. *E20* had fallen into a trap; some time earlier (in July 1915), the Germans had sunk the small French submarine *Mariotte*, and had captured some documents which revealed the places in the Marmara Sea where British and French submarines habitually made rendezvous. Despite setbacks such as this, and despite treacherous operating conditions, the British submariners achieved considerable success in the area. At the end of the war, the boats were assembled at Malta to await disposal.

SPECIFICATIONS

COUNTRY: United Kingdom
LAUNCH DATE: June 1915
CREW: 30
DISPLACEMENT: surfaced 677 tonnes (667 tons); submerged 820 tonnes (807 tons)
DIMENSIONS: 55.6m x 4.6m x 3.8m (182ft 5in x 15ft 1in x 12ft 6in)
ARMAMENT: five 457mm (18in) torpedo tubes; one 12-pounder gun
POWERPLANT: twin-screw diesel engines, electric motors
RANGE: 6035km (3579nm) at 10 knots
PERFORMANCE: surfaced 14 knots; submerged 9 knots

Enrico Tazzoli

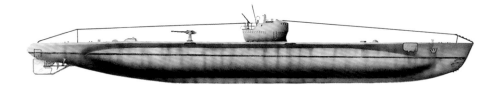

One of the four-strong Calvi class, *Enrico Tazzoli* was completed in 1936. She took part in the Spanish Civil War, and served in the Mediterranean in the early months after Italy's entry into World War II. In 1940, she transferred to the Atlantic, scoring an early success in October by sinking a 5217-tonne (5135-ton) freighter off the Portuguese coast. In December 1941, she was involved in a rescue operation in the Atlantic, ferrying part of the crew of the sunken commerce raider *Atlantis* to St Nazaire. In 1942, she was refitted to transport supplies to Japan. *Enrico Tazzoli* left Bordeaux on May 1943 and was never heard of again, being lost somewhere in the Bay of Biscay along with another Italian submarine, Barbarigo. Three more Italian boats that set out on a similar mission reached Sabang and Singapore without incident.

SPECIFICATIONS

COUNTRY: Italy
LAUNCH DATE: 14 October 1935
CREW: 77
DISPLACEMENT: surfaced 1574 tonnes (1500 tons); submerged 2092 tonnes (2060 tons)
DIMENSIONS: 84.3m x 7.7m x 5.2m (276ft 6in x 25ft 3in x 17ft 1in)
ARMAMENT: eight 533mm (21in) torpedo tubes; two 120mm (4.7in) guns
POWERPLANT: twin-screw diesel engines; electric motors
RANGE: 19,311km (10,409nm) at 10 knots
PERFORMANCE: surfaced 17 knots; submerged 8 knots

Enrico Toti

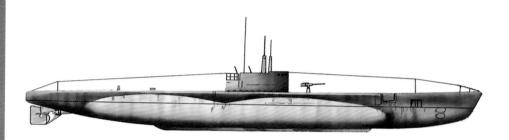

One of the Balilla class of large submarines, *Enrico Toti* was a long-range vessel with a diving depth of 90m (295ft). She served in the Spanish Civil War, and the early weeks of Italy's war found her operating against French shipping traffic evacuating troops and equipment from France to Algeria. Afterwards, *Enrico Toti* moved to a new operational area south of Crete. On 15 October 1940, off Calabria, she came upon the surfaced British submarine Rainbow and sank her in a gun duel. In the summer of 1942, it was decided that *Toti* was too large to operate offensively in the Mediterranean, and she spent some time in the transport role before being laid up in April 1943. Submarines of this class could carry a maximum of 16 torpedoes, and the class leader, *Balilla*, was equipped to carry four mines.

SPECIFICATIONS

COUNTRY: Italy
LAUNCH DATE: 14 April 1928
CREW: 76
DISPLACEMENT: surfaced 1473 tonnes (1450 tons); submerged 1934 tonnes (1904 tons)
DIMENSIONS: 87.7m x 7.8m x 4.7m (287ft 9in x 25ft 7in x 15ft 5in)
ARMAMENT: six 533mm (21in) torpedo tubes; one 120mm (4.7in) gun
POWERPLANT: twin-screw diesels, electric motors
RANGE: 7041km (3800nm) at 10 knots
PERFORMANCE: surfaced 17.5 knots; submerged 9 knots

Ersh (SHCH-303)

The Ersh (Pike) class of 88 boats, to which *Shch-303* belonged, were coastal submarines with a single hull and a maximum diving depth of 90m (295ft). Thirty-two were lost during World War II, but the survivors remained in service with the Soviet Navy until the mid-1950s. *Ersh Shch-303* operated in the Baltic, which was heavily mined and where most of the losses occurred; some of the Russian boats were sunk by Finnish submarines. The Russian submarines presented a great danger to the Germans, despite inflated claims of shipping sunk, and had to be guarded against at a cost that was unwelcome when German naval forces were badly needed elsewhere. *Shch-303*'s captain, I.V. Travkin, claimed to have sunk two large vessels in the Baltic, but the claim was never substantiated. *Shch-303* survived the war and was scrapped in 1958.

SPECIFICATIONS

COUNTRY: Russia
LAUNCH DATE: 16 November 1931
CREW: 45
DISPLACEMENT: surfaced 595 tonnes (586 tons); Ssbmerged: 713 tonnes (702 tons)
DIMENSIONS: 58.5m x 6.2m x 4.2m (192ft x 20ft 4in x 13ft 9in)
ARMAMENT: six 533mm (21in) torpedo tubes, two 45mm (1.8in) guns
POWERPLANT: twin-screw diesel engines, electric motors
RANGE: 11,112km (6000nm) at 8 knots
PERFORMANCE: surfaced 12.5 knots; submerged 8.5 knots

Espadon (1901)

Espadon (*Swordfish*) was one of France's earliest submarines, and was very much an experimental craft, being used for various trials. The big problem facing early submarine designers was how to propel the boat. Trials with compressed air were successful, but the storage space this required was too great to achieve reasonable speed and range. By the 1880s, steam power was being used on the surface, the machinery being shut down in order to engage the newly introduced electric motors for submersion. *Espadon* was one of this type of submarine. She was removed from the effective list in 1919. The French were very innovative in their early submarine designs, and were not afraid to experiment with novel forms of propulsion and other technological aspects of underwater craft.

SPECIFICATIONS

COUNTRY: France
LAUNCH DATE: September 1901
CREW: 30
DISPLACEMENT: surfaced 159 tonnes (157 tons); submerged 216 tonnes (213 tons)
DIMENSIONS: 32.5m x 3.9m x 2.5m (106ft 8in x 12ft 10in x 8ft 2in)
ARMAMENT: four 450mm (17.7in) torpedoes
POWERPLANT: single-screw triple-expansion steam engine; electric motor
RANGE: 1111km (600nm) at 8 knots
PERFORMANCE: surfaced 9.75 knots; submerged 8 knots

Espadon (1926)

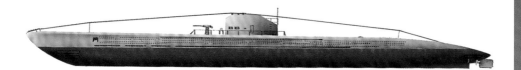

The French produced some very capable submarines in the interwar years. *Espadon* (*Swordfish*) belonged to the Requin (Shark) class of nine minelaying submarines that were designated First Class Submarines by the French Admiralty. They were heavily armed, with four bow, two stern and two twin torpedo tubes mounted in containers in the upper hull. All ships of the class were modernized, undergoing a complete refit of hull and machinery between 1935 and 1937. Eight of the group were lost during World War II. *Requin*, *Dauphin*, *Phoque* and *Espadon* were seized by the Italians at Bizerta on 8 December 1942. *Espadon* was towed to Castellamare di Stabia and was given the designation *FR114* by her captors, but was not commissioned into the Italian Navy. She was captured by the Germans and scuttled on 13 September 1943.

SPECIFICATIONS

COUNTRY: France
LAUNCH DATE: 28 May 1926
CREW: 54
DISPLACEMENT: surfaced 1168 tonnes (1150 tons); submerged 1464 tonnes (1441 tons)
DIMENSIONS: 78.2m x 6.8m x 5m (256ft 9in x 22ft 5in x 16ft 9in)
ARMAMENT: ten 533mm (21in) torpedo tubes; one 100mm (3.9in) gun
POWERPLANT: twin-screw diesel engines; electric motors
RANGE: 10,469km (5650nm) at 10 knots
PERFORMANCE: surfaced 15 knots; submerged 9 knots

Ettore Fieramosca

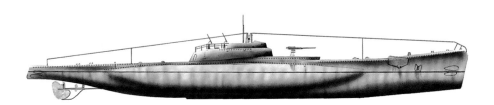

W hen Italy entered the war in June 1940, no fewer than 84 submarines were operational; the remainder of the 150 boats commissioned were either in refit or undergoing trials. They were markedly inferior to all German U-boats, comfort playing too great a part in their design. Their conning towers were overlarge, partly because they contained a big, well-equipped galley! In the main they were large, good-looking vessels, but they were slow to dive, clumsy when submerged and poorly equipped. *Ettore Fieramosca* was no exception. She was in a class of her own, designed for long-range ocean patrols. To this end, provision was made for her to carry a small reconnaissance aircraft in a hangar at the rear of the conning tower, but the aircraft was never embarked. The submarine was laid up in March 1941.

SPECIFICATIONS
COUNTRY: Italy
LAUNCH DATE: April 1929
CREW: 78
DISPLACEMENT: surfaced 1580 tonnes (1556 tons); submerged 1996 tonnes (1965 tons)
DIMENSIONS: 84m x 8.3m x 5.3m (275ft 7in x 27ft 3in x 17ft 5in)
ARMAMENT: eight 533mm (21in) torpedo tubes; one 120mm (4.7in) gun
POWERPLANT: twin-screw diesel engines; electric motors
RANGE: 9260km (5000nm) at 9 knots
PERFORMANCE: surfaced 19 knots; submerged 10 knots

Euler

Thanks to a small number of far-sighted naval officers and politicians, France had built up a formidable submarine fleet when World War I broke out; indeed, by comparison with Germany and the United Kingdom, her submarine arm was extraordinarily large. Much of the reason for this lay in the fact that she felt it necessary to keep pace in naval developments with her neighbour, the UK. As she could not match the latter in capital ship strength her naval planners tended to concentrate on building submarines and torpedo boats, in other words, vessels that could inflict massive damage on larger ships at a relatively low cost. *Euler* formed part of a large class of 16 boats. Her submerged range was 160km (86nm) at 5 knots. She was removed from the effective list in the 1920s.

SPECIFICATIONS

COUNTRY: France
LAUNCH DATE: October 1912
CREW: 35
DISPLACEMENT: surfaced 403 tonnes (397 tons); submerged 560 tonnes (551 tons)
DIMENSIONS: 52m x 5.4m x 3m (170ft 1in x 17ft 9in x 10ft 3in)
ARMAMENT: one 450mm (17.7in) torpedo tube, four drop collars, two external cradles
POWERPLANT: twin-screw diesel engines, electric motors
RANGE: 3230km (1741nm) at 10 knots
PERFORMANCE: surfaced 14 knots; submerged 7 knots

Eurydice

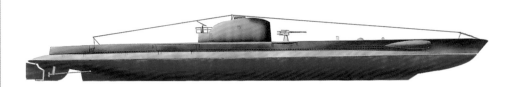

Eurydice was a double-hulled, medium-displacement submarine with an operational diving depth of 80m (262ft). She formed part of a class of 26 second-class boats built between 1925 and 1934 and was in fact one of a batch of three built at the Normand-Fenaux yard. When Italy entered the war in June 1940 *Eurydice* was at Oran, and immediately began defensive patrols off Gibraltar together with other French submarines. This was in accordance with an Anglo-French naval agreement under which the French Navy had responsibility for the defence of the western Mediterranean, an agreement that came to nothing with the Franco-German Armistice of June 1940. *Eurydice* was scuttled at Toulon on 27 November 1942 along with many other French warships, shortly before the port was occupied by II SS Panzer Corps in Operation *Lila*.

SPECIFICATIONS

COUNTRY: France
LAUNCH DATE: May 1927
CREW: 41
DISPLACEMENT: surfaced 636 tonnes (626 tons); submerged 800 tonnes (787 tons)
DIMENSIONS: 65.9m x 4.9m x 4m (216ft 2in x 16ft 1in x 13ft 1in)
ARMAMENT: seven 533mm (21in) torpedo tubes
POWERPLANT: twin-screw diesel engines; electric motors
RANGE: 6485km (3500nm) at 7.7 knots
PERFORMANCE: surfaced 14 knots; submerged 7.5 knots

F1 (1915)

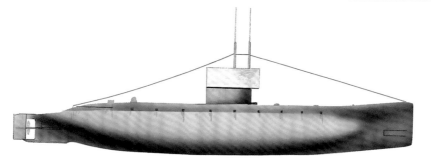

F1 was one of a class of three vessels which were among the last coastal-defence submarines built for the Royal Navy, due to the Admiralty's decision to adopt an offensive policy by building ocean-going submarines of great range. The policy was encouraged by Winston Churchill, who became First Lord of the Admiralty in 1911, and observed that of the 57 submarines then in service with the Royal Navy, only two D-class boats were capable of operating at anything more than a short distance from Britain's shores. By the end of 1914, it had become clear that enemy submarine commanders did not intend to pursue British ships into their harbours. *F1* was laid down in 1913, and all three boats in the class saw extensive service during World War I. A proposed group of boats in the same class was cancelled in 1914. *F1* was broken up in 1920.

SPECIFICATIONS

COUNTRY: United Kingdom
LAUNCH DATE: March 1915
CREW: 20
DISPLACEMENT: surfaced 368 tonnes (363 tons); submerged 533 tonnes (525 tons)
DIMENSIONS: 46m x 4.9m x 3.2m (151ft x 16ft 1in x 10ft 6in)
ARMAMENT: three 457mm (18in) torpedo tubes
POWERPLANT: twin-screw diesel engines; electric motors
RANGE: 5556km (3000nm) at 9 knots
PERFORMANCE: turfaced: 14 knots; submerged: 8.7 knots

F1 (1916)

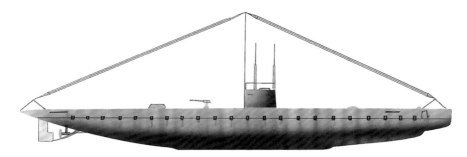

F1 and her sisters were improved versions of the Medusa class. They were able to dive faster and carried two periscopes (one for search, the other for attack), as well as a gyrocompass and the newly invented Fessenden submarine-signalling apparatus. *F1* was removed from the effective list in June 1930. Experience with craft such as *F1* should have made the Italian submarine service a sound and effective service, but between the wars it seems to have existed more for show than action. There is scant evidence of realistic pre-World War II submarine exercises, and the very special teamwork demanded of an aggressive submarine crew appears to have been lacking. In both world wars, it was the Italian torpedo-boat crews who were the most consistently aggressive in combat. On one occasion, they made a gallant attempt to attack British shipping in Malta.

SPECIFICATIONS

COUNTRY: Italy
LAUNCH DATE: April 1916
CREW: 54
DISPLACEMENT: surfaced 226 tonnes (262 tons); submerged 324 tonnes (319 tons)
DIMENSIONS: 45.6m x 4.2m x 3m (149ft 7in x 13ft 9in x 9ft 10in)
ARMAMENT: two 450mm (17.7in) torpedo tubes; one 76mm (3in) gun
POWERPLANT: twin-screw diesel engines; electric motors
RANGE: 2963km (1600nm) at 8.5 knots
PERFORMANCE: surfaced 12.5 knots; submerged 8.2 knots

F4

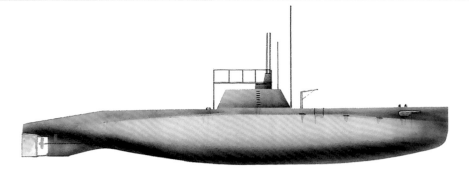

F4 and her three sisters were similar to – and contemporaries of – the E class, where a tendency towards a smaller type of submarine had originated. All the E- and F-class boats were withdrawn from service in 1915 for re-engineering. F4 left Honolulu harbour on 25 March 1915 for a short trial run, but she never returned. She was located at a depth of 91 metres (300ft) just off Pearl Harbor, well beyond the depth from which such a vessel had hitherto been successfully raised. Five months later, however, American salvage crews achieved the seemingly impossible and brought F4 to the surface, setting up a new world deep-sea diving record in the process. In the years to come America remained at the forefront of such salvage operations, with specially-designed deep submergence craft.

SPECIFICATIONS

COUNTRY: United States
LAUNCH DATE: January 1912
CREW: 35
DISPLACEMENT: surfaced 335 tonnes (330 tons); submerged 406 tonnes (400 tons)
DIMENSIONS: 43.5m x 4.7m x 3.7m (142ft 9in x 15ft 5in x 12ft 2in)
ARMAMENT: four torpedo tubes
POWERPLANT: twin-screw diesels, electric motors
RANGE: 4260km (2300nm) at 11 knots
PERFORMANCE: surfaced 13.5 knots; submerged 5 knots

Faà di Bruno

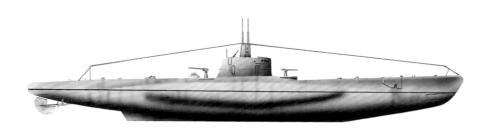

Derived from the Glauco class, the *Faa di Bruno* was a long-range, single-hulled, ocean-going boat with internal ballast tanks designed by Bernardis. There were two boats in the class, the other being the *Commandante Cappellini*. In November 1940, the *Faa di Bruno* was sunk in the North Atlantic through an unknown cause, but possibly by the British destroyer HMS *Havelock*. Her sister, *Cappellini*, had an interesting career. Converted to the transport role, she was captured by the Japanese at Sabang in September 1943, following the Italian armistice, and turned over to the Germans. By 1944, long-range submarines provided the only means of shipping raw materials between Germany and Japan. When Germany capitulated in May 1945, the Japanese seized her again and gave her the serial *I-503*. She ended the war at Kobe, Japan, and was scrapped in 1946.

SPECIFICATIONS

COUNTRY: Italy
LAUNCH DATE: 18 June 1939
CREW: 58
DISPLACEMENT: surfaced 1076 tonnes (1060 tons); submerged 1334 tonnes (1313 tons)
DIMENSIONS: 73m x 7m x 5m (239ft 6in x 23ft 7in x 16ft 9in)
ARMAMENT: eight 533mm (21in) torpedo tubes; two 100mm (3.9in) guns
POWERPLANT: twin-screw diesel engines; electric motors
RANGE: 13,890km (7500nm) at 9.4 knots
PERFORMANCE: surfaced 17.4 knots; submerged 8 knots

Farfadet

arfadet and her three sisters relied solely on a set of accumulators for power, which gave them a range of only 218.5km (118nm) at 5.3 knots surfaced and 53km (28.5nm) at 4.3 knots submerged. The four torpedoes were carried externally in cradles aft of the conning tower. As a result of the conning tower hatch being left open, *Farfadet* sank at Bizerta on 6 July 1905, with the loss of 14 lives. She was subsequently raised and recommissioned as *Follet* in 1909. She was removed from the effective list in 1913. *Farfadet* was yet another example of French attempts to find alternative, cleaner power sources for their early submarines. French designers were extremely safety-conscious, and refused for the most part to countenance volatile petrol engines. The initial cost of each boat in this class was £32,000 (US$51,200).

SPECIFICATIONS

COUNTRY: France
LAUNCH DATE: May 1901
CREW: 25
DISPLACEMENT: surfaced 188 tonnes (185 tons); submerged 205 tonnes (202 tons)
DIMENSIONS: 41.3m x 2.9m x 2.6m (135ft 6in x 9ft 6in x 8ft 6in)
ARMAMENT: four 450mm (17.7in) torpedo tubes
POWERPLANT: single screw; electric motors
RANGE: 218.5km (118nm) at 5.3 knots
PERFORMANCE: surfaced 6 knots; submerged 4.3 knots

Fenian Ram

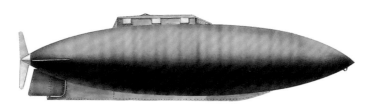

The Irish-American inventor John Philip Holland designed submarines in America, the original idea being to use them to destroy the hated British fleet on behalf of his fellow Fenians. Ironically, his business acumen overcame his nationalist sympathies and he sold his most successful design to the Royal Navy. Twenty years earlier, the *Fenian Ram* was built for the Fenian Society by the Delamater Iron Works in New York. In 1883, she was towed to Newhaven under great secrecy, so that her crew of three could familiarize themselves with her handling. The vessel was exhibited at Madison Square Gardens in 1916 in order to raise funds for the Irish uprising that took place that year. In 1927, the *Fenian Ram* was housed in West Side Park, New York. John Holland has a firm place in history as the designer of the first practical submarines.

SPECIFICATIONS

COUNTRY: United States
LAUNCH DATE: May 1881
CREW: 3
DISPLACEMENT: surfaced 19 tonnes (19 tons); submerged not known
DIMENSIONS: 9.4m x 1.8m x 2.2m (30ft 10in x 5ft 11in x 7ft 3in)
ARMAMENT: one 228mm (9in) gun
POWERPLANT: single-screw petrol engine
RANGE: not known
PERFORMANCE: not known

Ferraris

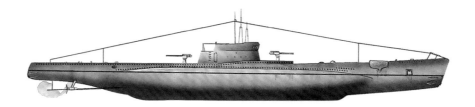

Ferraris and her sister *Galilei* were long range vessels with a partial double hull. Both boats took part in the Spanish Civil War, as did two others of the class, *Archimede* and *Torricelli*. These two were transferred to Spain in Spring 1937, being respectively named *General Sanjurjo* and *General Mola*. *Ferraris* and *Galilei* were stationed in the Red Sea at the time of Italy's entry into World War II. *Galilei* was captured in the Red Sea on 19 October 1940 after a surface battle with the British armed trawler *Moonstone* in which nearly all the Italian officers were killed, and the rest of the crew inside the boat were poisoned by emissions from the air-conditioning system. The *Ferraris* was designated *X2* by the British and used for training. She was sunk in the North Adriatic by the British destroyer *Lamerton* in October 1941.

SPECIFICATIONS
COUNTRY: Italy
LAUNCH DATE: August 1934
CREW: 55
DISPLACEMENT: surfaced 1000 tonnes (985 tons); submerged 1279 tonnes (1259 tons)
DIMENSIONS: 70.5m x 6.8m x 4m (231ft 4in x 22ft 4in x 13ft 1in)
ARMAMENT: eight 533mm (21in) torpedo tubes; two 100mm (3.9in) guns
POWERPLANT: twin-screw diesel engines
RANGE: 19,446km (10,500nm) at 8 knots
PERFORMANCE: surfaced 17 knots; submerged 8.5 knots

Filippo Corridoni

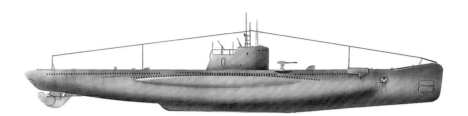

Filippo Corridoni was a short-range minelayer, one of two submarines – the other was the *Brigadin* – developed from the Pisano class. She was used mainly to transport supplies during World War II. The vessels carried two tubes for launching mines; between 16 and 24 of the latter could be carried, depending on the type. Some 17 different types of mine were used by the Italian Navy in World War II, including one known as the Coloniale P125 developed specifically for use in warm seas. The Italians also used German mines from 1941; these were generally more effective than the Italian models. The Italian Navy placed great faith in mines, and many boats of their submarine fleet were converted to the minelaying role. The *Filippo Corridoni* was removed from the effective list in 1948, as was the *Brigadin*.

SPECIFICATIONS
COUNTRY: Italy
LAUNCH DATE: March 1930
CREW: 55
DISPLACEMENT: surfaced 996 tonnes (981 tons); submerged 1185 tonnes (1167 tons)
DIMENSIONS: 71.5m x 6m x 4.8m (234ft 7in x 20ft 2in x 15ft 9in)
ARMAMENT: four 533mm (21in) torpedo tubes; one 102mm (4in) gun; up to 24 mines
POWERPLANT: twin-screw diesel engines, electric motors
RANGE: 16,668km (9000nm) at 8 knots
PERFORMANCE: surfaced 11.5 knots; submerged 7 knots

Foca (1908)

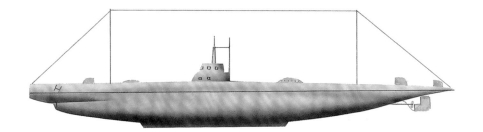

Foca was the only Italian submarine to have three shafts, driven by three sets of FIAT petrol engines. On 26 April 1909, in Naples harbour, an internal petrol explosion set fire to her fuel and she was scuttled to prevent the blaze spreading. She was later raised, repaired, and the central motor with its shaft and propeller were removed. The accident underlined the dangers inherent in using petrol engines in submersible craft, whose interiors quickly filled with volatile vapour that could easily be ignited by a chance spark, with disastrous consequences. After this accident the Italian Navy gave up building petrol-powered submarines. The early British boats had suffered similar problems, leading to the rapid adoption of diesel engines as the primary power source. *Foca* was finally discarded in September 1918, as World War I drew to a close.

SPECIFICATIONS

COUNTRY: Italy
LAUNCH DATE: September 1908
CREW: 2 + 15
DISPLACEMENT: surfaced 188 tonnes (185 tons); submerged 284 tonnes (280 tons)
DIMENSIONS: 42.5m x 4.3m x 2.6m (139ft 5in x 14ft 1in x 8ft 7in)
ARMAMENT: two 450mm (17.7in) torpedo tubes
POWERPLANT: petrol engines, electric motors
RANGE: not known
PERFORMANCE: not known

Foca (1937)

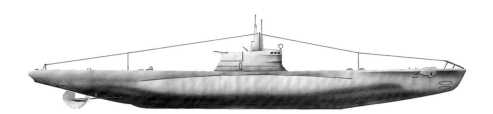

Foca was one of three minelaying submarines built for the Italian Navy just before World War II, the others being *Atropo* and *Zoea*. As first completed, their 100mm (3.9in) gun was mounted in a training turret, in the after part of the conning tower. This gun was later removed and mounted in the traditional deck position, forward of the conning tower. Torpedo armament was sacrificed to provide two mine chutes at the stern. The class leader, *Foca*, was lost on 15 October 1940 while laying a mine barrage off Haifa, Palestine; it was thought that she had probably run into a British minefield. *Atropo* and *Zoea* survived the war and were discarded in 1947. Late in 1943, *Atropo* was used by the Allies to run supplies to British garrisons on the Aegean islands of Samos and Leros; the Aegean was heavily patrolled by enemy MTBs, and this was the safest method.

SPECIFICATIONS

COUNTRY: Italy
LAUNCH DATE: 26 June 1937
CREW: 60
DISPLACEMENT: surfaced 1354 tonnes (1333 tons); submerged 1685 tonnes (1659 tons)
DIMENSIONS: 82.8m x 7.2m x 5.3m (271ft 8in x 23ft 6in x 17ft 5in)
ARMAMENT: six 533mm (21in) torpedo tubes; one 100mm (3.9in) gun
POWERPLANT: twin-screw diesel engines, electric motors
RANGE: 15,742km (8500nm) at 8 knots
PERFORMANCE: surfaced 15.2 knots; submerged 7.4 knots

Francesco Rismondo

Francesco Rismondo was the former Yugoslav submarine *Ostvenik* (N1), captured on 17 April 1941 at Cattaro by the Italian Navy. She was one of two Yugoslav boats built by Ateliers et Chantiers de la Loire at Nantes; the other was the *Smeli* (N2), which was captured at the same time. A third boat, also taken by the Italians at Cattaro, was the Vickers-built *Hrabri* (N3), whose sister ship *Nebojsa* succeeded in getting away before the Italians occupied Dalmatia. *Francesco Rismondo* was captured by German forces at Bonifacio on 14 September 1943, following the Italian armistice with the Allies, and sunk by them at the same port four days later. After the war, the Italian submarine *Nautilo* was awarded to the Yugoslav Navy as war booty, serving as the *Sava* until 1970.

SPECIFICATIONS

COUNTRY: Italy
LAUNCH DATE: 14 February 1929
CREW: 45
DISPLACEMENT: surfaced 676 tonnes (665 tons); submerged 835 tonnes (822 tons)
DIMENSIONS: 66.5m x 5.4m x 3.8m (218ft 2in x17ft 9in x 12ft 4in)
ARMAMENT: six 551mm (21.7in) torpedo tubes; one 100mm (3.9in) gun
POWERPLANT: two diesel engines, two electric motors
RANGE: 5003km (2700nm) at 10 knots
PERFORMANCE: surfaced 14.5 knots; submerged 9.2 knots

Fratelli Bandiera

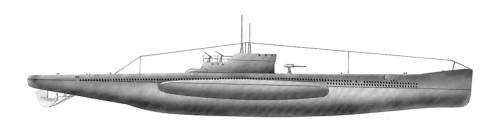

Fratelli Bandiera was leader of a class of four, the others being the *Luciano Manara*, *Ciro Menotti* and *Santorre Santarosa*. The latter was torpedoed by the British *MTB 260* on 20 January 1943, having run aground off Tripoli; she was eventually scuttled. Initially, the boats of this class had a maximum speed of 17.9 knots on the surface and just over 9 knots when submerged. They tended to plunge into oncoming waves, however, and this poor stability made it necessary to mount bulges on either side of the hull, creating extra drag. The engineer responsible for this class was Curio Bernardis. Bandiera, Manara and Menotti were used for training and transport duties in World War II, undergoing some modifications that included the raising of the bow and a reduction in size of the conning tower. All were discarded in 1948.

SPECIFICATIONS

COUNTRY: Italy
LAUNCH DATE: 07 August 1929
CREW: 52
DISPLACEMENT: surfaced 880 tonnes (866 tons); submerged 1114 tonnes (1096 tons)
DIMENSIONS: 69.8m x 7.2m x 5.2m (229ft x 23ft 8in x 17ft 1in)
ARMAMENT: eight 533mm (21in) torpedo tubes; one 100mm (3.9in) gun
POWERPLANT: two sets of diesel engines, two electric motors
RANGE: 8797km (4750nm) at 8.5 knots
PERFORMANCE: surfaced 15.1 knots; submerged 8.2 knots

Frimaire

Frimaire was one of the Brumaire class of 16 submarines launched in 1911–13. All 16 boats operated in the Mediterranean during World War I. One of them, *Bernouilli*, infiltrated Cattaro harbour on 4 April 1916 and torpedoed the Austrian destroyer *Csepel*, blowing off her stern. Another, *Le Verrier*, accidentally rammed the German *U47* on 28 July 1918 after an unsuccessful torpedo engagement. Three were lost; *Fourcault* was sunk off Cattaro by Austrian aircraft, *Curie* was captured at Pola after becoming trapped in the harbour and recommissioned by the Austrians as the *U14* (she was recovered by the French at the end of the war) and *Joule* was mined in the Dardanelles. *Frimaire* was stricken from the navy list in 1923. The boats of this class were all named after the months of the French Revolutionary calendar.

SPECIFICATIONS

COUNTRY: France
LAUNCH DATE: 26 August 1911
CREW: 29
DISPLACEMENT: surfaced 403 tonnes (397 tons); submerged 560 tonnes (551 tons)
DIMENSIONS: 52.1m x 5.14m x 3.1m (170ft 11in x 17ft 9in x 10ft 2in)
ARMAMENT: six 450mm (17.7in) torpedo tubes
POWERPLANT: two-shaft diesel engines, electric motors
RANGE: 3150km (1700nm) at 10 knots
PERFORMANCE: surfaced 13 knots; submerged 8 knots

Fulton

Fulton was laid down at Cherbourg in late 1913, but was not completed until July 1920 because other types of warship were allocated a higher priority in the French naval construction programme. *Fulton* was originally designed with two 2000hp turbines, altered to diesel machinery in the course of construction. The submarine was named after the American Robert Fulton, designer of France's first submersible (the *Nautilus)*, which was launched in 1800. An ardent pacifist, Fulton's desire was to build submarines to destroy the world's battle fleets; but the submarine was then far too crude to influence naval warfare and was doomed to remain little more than a toy for a century, more lethal to its operator than the enemy. It took another American, John Holland, to design a practical submersible.

SPECIFICATIONS

COUNTRY: France
LAUNCH DATE: April 1919
CREW: 45
DISPLACEMENT: surfaced 884 tonnes (870 tons); submerged 1267 tonnes (1247 tons)
DIMENSIONS: 74m x 6.4m x 3.6m (242ft 9in x 21ft x 11ft 10in)
ARMAMENT: eight 450mm (17.7in) torpedo tubes; two 75mm (3in) guns
POWERPLANT: twin-screw diesel engines; electric motors
RANGE: 7964km (4300nm) at 10 knots
PERFORMANCE: surfaced not known; submerged not known

G1

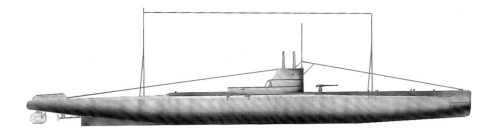

The G class of 14 boats, based on the E class design, was ordered by the British Admiralty in 1914 in response to information that Germany was about to build a fleet of double-hulled, oceangoing submarines. Two of the G class boats were lost in action during World War I and two more through accidental causes. One of their main tasks during the war was to ambush U-boats trying to pass through the Channel. The boats had an unusual armament arrangement in that they were fitted with torpedo tubes of different calibres: one 533mm (21in) and four 457mm (18in) torpedo tubes, the larger-calibre weapon being intended for use against armoured targets. One G-class boat, *G7*, had the unhappy distinction of being the last British submarine lost in World War I, failing to return from a North Sea patrol on 1 November 1918.

SPECIFICATIONS

COUNTRY: United Kingdom
LAUNCH DATE: August 1915
CREW: 31
DISPLACEMENT: surfaced 704 tonnes (693 tons); submerged 850 tonnes (836 tons)
DIMENSIONS: 57m x 6.9m x 4.1m (187ft x 22ft 7in x 13ft 6in)
ARMAMENT: four 457mm (18in) torpedo tubes, one 533mm (21in) torpedo tube, one 76mm (3in) gun
POWERPLANT: twin-screw diesel-electric motors
RANGE: 4445km (2400nm) at 12.5 knots
PERFORMANCE: surfaced 14.25 knots; submerged 9 knots

Galatea

Galatea was one of 12 boats of the Sirena class, which was an improvement on the basic '600' design with improved seakeeping qualities, higher speed and better handling when submerged. Many of the 12 boats underwent modifications during their careers and, during the Spanish civil war, Sirena-class boats carried out 18 extended patrols. The boats could carry a total of 12 533mm (21in) torpedoes, and their AA armament was gradually upgraded as the Second World War progressed. From 1940–43 they saw action in the Mediterranean, and all but *Galatea* were war losses. One of them, *Topazio*, was sunk in error by RAF aircraft south-east of Sardinia four days after Italy concluded an armistice with the Allies, the cause being lack of identification signals from the submarine. *Galatea* was discarded in February 1948.

SPECIFICATIONS

COUNTRY: Italy
LAUNCH DATE: 5 October 1933
CREW: 45
DISPLACEMENT: surfaced 690 tonnes (679 tons); submerged 775 tonnes (701 tons)
DIMENSIONS: 60.2m x 6.5m x 4.6m (197ft 5in x 21ft 2in x 15ft 1in)
ARMAMENT: six 533mm (21in) torpedo tubes; one 100mm (3.9in) gun
POWERPLANT: twin-screw diesel/electric motors
RANGE: 9260km (5000nm) at 8 knots
PERFORMANCE: surfaced 14 knots; submerged 7.7 knots

Galathée

On the outbreak of World War II, the group of medium-range submarines to which *Galathée* belonged was the largest class of such vessels in the French Navy, and they operated intensively until the French collapse in June 1940. *Galathée* was one of a batch of three boats built by Ateliers Loire-Simonot; they were laid down in 1923 and completed in 1927. In spite of having a complex torpedo layout, involving a double revolving mounting, *Galathée* and her consorts were successful ships. She was scuttled at Toulon on 27 November 1942, shortly before the harbour was occupied by troops of the II SS-Panzer Corps; this action followed the Allied landings in North Africa earlier in the month. Most of the boats that remained under the control of Vichy France lay idle from June 1940 to the end of 1942.

SPECIFICATIONS

COUNTRY: France
LAUNCH DATE: 18 December 1925
CREW: 41
DISPLACEMENT: surfaced 619 tonnes (609 tons); submerged 769 tonnes (757 tons)
DIMENSIONS: 64m x 5.2m x 4.3m (210ft x 17ft x 14ft 1in)
ARMAMENT: seven 551mm (21.7in) torpedo tubes; one 76mm (3in) gun
POWERPLANT: twin-screw diesel/electric motors
RANGE: 6485km (3500nm) at 7.5 knots
PERFORMANCE: surfaced 13.5 knots; submerged 7.5 knots

Galilei

The two Archimede-class submarines *Galilei* and *Ferraris* both served in the Spanish Civil War and, when Italy entered World War II, they were both in the Red Sea at Massawa. On the outbreak of hostilities, *Ferraris* set up a patrol area off Djibouti and *Galilei* an area off Aden. On 16 June 1940, *Galilei* sank the Norwegian tanker *James Stove*. Two days later, she stopped the Yugoslav steamer *Drava* but had to release her; on the following day she was sighted by the armed British anti-submarine trawler *Moonstone* and a gun battle ensured in which nearly all her officers were killed and the crew, still below, were poisoned by emissions from the air-conditioning system. She was captured and forced into British service as the *P711*. She was used as a training boat in the East Indies and Mediterranean, and was scrapped in 1946.

SPECIFICATIONS

COUNTRY: Italy
LAUNCH DATE: 9 March 1934
CREW: 55
DISPLACEMENT: surfaced 1001 tonnes (985 tons); submerged 1279 tonnes (1259 tons)
DIMENSIONS: 70.5m x 6.8m x 4.1m (231ft 4in x 22ft 4in x 13ft 5in)
ARMAMENT: eight 533mm (21in) torpedo tubes; two 100mm (3.9in) guns
POWERPLANT: twin-screw diesel/electric motors
RANGE: 6670km (3600nm) at 10 knots
PERFORMANCE: surfaced 17 knots; submerged 8.5 knots

Galvani

Galvani was one of three Brin-class submarines. On 10 June 1940, at the point of Italy's entry into the war, she was in the Red Sea under Cdr Spano. With the commencement of hostilities, *Galvani* set up a patrol area in the Gulf of Oman, where she sank an Indian sloop, HMIS *Pathan*. Her fate was sealed, however, by the capture of the *Galilei*, whose documents revealed the location of all Indian submarines in the Red Sea area. On 24 June, she was located by British warships, which opened fire on her. She was finished off by depth charges from the sloop HMS *Falmouth*. Her sister ship and third of the class, *Guglielmotti*, was sunk off Calabria on 17 March 1942 by torpedoes from HMS *Unbeaten*. The class leader, *Brin*, went on to see much service as a training boat in the Indian ocean after Italy's armistice with the Allies.

SPECIFICATIONS

COUNTRY: Italy
LAUNCH DATE: 22 May 1938
CREW: 58
DISPLACEMENT: surfaced 1032 tonnes (1016 tons); submerged 1286 tonnes (1266 tons)
DIMENSIONS: 72.4m x 6.9m x 4.5m (237ft 6in x 22ft 8in x 14ft 11in)
ARMAMENT: eight 533mm (21in) torpedo tubes; one 100mm (3.9in) gun
POWERPLANT: twin-screw diesel/electric motors
RANGE: 19,446km (10,500nm) at 8 knots
PERFORMANCE: surfaced 17.3 knots; submerged 8 knots

Gemma

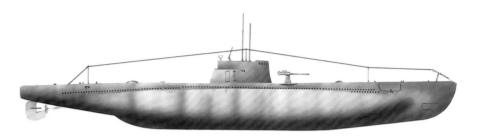

L aid down in September 1935 and completed in July 1936, *Gemma* was one of a class of ten short-range boats of the Perla class, derived in turn from the Sirena series that had been completed in 1933–34, but with a slight increase in displacement and more modern equipment. Project designer for this class was General Engineer Curio Bernardis. Their maximum diving depth was 70–80m (230–260ft). They undertook patrols on behalf of the Nationalists in the Spanish Civil War, and two were ceded to Spain for several months. Five were lost in World War II, including *Gemma*. Her early war patrol station was off Sollum in the eastern Mediterranean. She was later transferred to the south-eastern approaches to the Aegean, where, on 6 October 1940, she was sunk in error by the Italian submarine *Tricheco*.

SPECIFICATIONS

COUNTRY: Italy
LAUNCH DATE: 21 May 1936
CREW: 45
DISPLACEMENT: surfaced 711 tonnes (700 tons); submerged 711 tonnes (830 tons)
DIMENSIONS: 60.2m x 6.5m x 4.6m (197ft 5in x 21ft 2in x 15ft 1in)
ARMAMENT: six 533mm (21in) torpedo tubes; one 100mm (3.9in) gun
POWERPLANT: twin-screw diesel/electric motors
RANGE: 9260km (5000nm) at 8 knots
PERFORMANCE: surfaced 14 knots; submerged 7.5 knots

General Mola

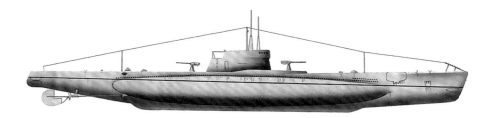

General Mola was formerly the Italian submarine *Torricelli*, which was transferred to Spain in 1937 together with the *Archimede*. To cover up the deal, the Italians built two more submarines in conditions of the strictest secrecy and gave them the same names. The two vessels remained on the Spanish Navy's inventory until the early 1950s, when they were replaced by two locally-built D-class submarines. *General Mola* bore the pennant number *C5* from 1950 until she was stricken in 1959. As a matter of interest, Spain also used an ex-German Type VII U-boat until the 1960s (the *U573*), damaged by a Hudson aircraft of the RAF east of Gibraltar on 1 May 1942 and forced to seek refuge in a Spanish port, where she was interned. She was purchased from Germany in the following year and given the number *G7*.

SPECIFICATIONS

COUNTRY: Spain
LAUNCH DATE: April 1934
CREW: 55
DISPLACEMENT: surfaced 1001 tonnes (985 tons); submerged 1279 tonnes (1259 tons)
DIMENSIONS: 70.5m x 6.8m x 4.1m (231ft 4in x 22ft 4in x 13ft 5in)
ARMAMENT: eight 533mm (21in) torpedo tubes; two 100mm (3.9in) guns
POWERPLANT: twin-screw diesel/electric motors
RANGE: 6670km (3600nm) at 10 knots
PERFORMANCE: surfaced 17 knots; submerged 8.5 knots

Giacinto Pullino

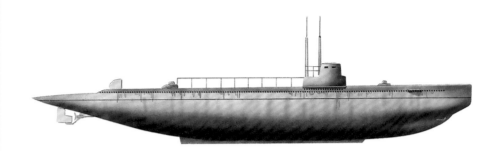

Giacinto Pullino was laid down at La Spezia dockyard in June 1912 and was completed in December 1913. During World War I, she served in the Adriatic, along with most other Italian submarines of the time, where her main function was to carry out frequent reconnaissance missions along the Dalmatian coast, which was held by the Austro-Hungarians and whose many harbours and inlets provided refuges for their warships. Because of the relatively shallow waters of the Adriatic's east coast it was difficult and dangerous work, and it was during one such mission in July 1916 that Giacinto Pullino ran aground on Galiola Island, Quarnaro, and was seized by Austrian forces. She sank while being towed to Pola on 1 August 1917. In 1931 the Italian Navy raised her, but she was scrapped later the same year.

SPECIFICATIONS

COUNTRY: Italy
LAUNCH DATE: July 1913
CREW: 40
DISPLACEMENT: surfaced 350 tonnes (345 tons); submerged 411 tonnes (405 tons)
DIMENSIONS: 42.2m x 4m x 3.7m (138ft 6in x 13ft 1in x 12ft 4in)
ARMAMENT: six 450mm (17.7in) torpedo tubes; one 57mm (2.25in) and one 47mm (1.85in) guns
POWERPLANT: twin-screw diesel/electric motors
RANGE: not known
PERFORMANCE: surfaced 14 knots; submerged 9 knots

Giacomo Nani

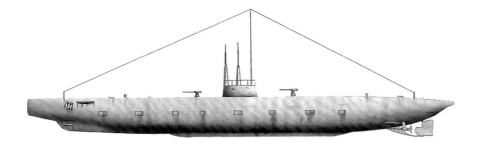

Giacomo Nani and her three sisters were fast, medium-sized submarines designed by Laurenti and Cavallini. *Giacomo Nani* was laid down in 1915, but was not completed in time to see service in World War I, where her superior speed – both surfaced and dived – would certainly have made her a formidable opponent. She was stricken from the Navy list in 1935, by which time the Italian Navy had several new classes of submarine on its inventory. Not all of them were as well designed as *Giacomo Nani*; the early pre-war classes of submarine in Italian service had numerous problems, mostly concerned with underwater handling, and were constantly modified to improve matters. Much of the design expertise built up during World War I had been lost when shipyards came under state control after 1925.

SPECIFICATIONS

COUNTRY: Italy
LAUNCH DATE: September 1918
CREW: 35
DISPLACEMENT: surfaced 774 tonnes (762 tons); submerged 938 tonnes (924 tons)
DIMENSIONS: 67m x 5.9m x 3.8m (220ft x 19ft 4in x 12ft 6in)
ARMAMENT: six 450mm (17.7in) torpedo tubes; two 76mm (3in) guns
POWERPLANT: twin-screw diesel/electric motors
RANGE: not known
PERFORMANCE: surfaced 16 knots; submerged 10 knots

Giovanni Bausan

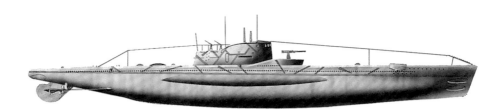

Giovanni Bausan was one of four submarines of the Pisani class laid down in 1925–26. This class of submarine was a joint design project between Colonel Engineer Curio Bernardis and Major Engineer Tizzoni. She was a short-range boat with an internal double hull. Because of stability problems revealed during trials, all four boats in the class were fitted with external bulges, which reduced their speed by about 2 knots on the surface and 1 knot submerged. In 1940 Giovanni Bausan became a training ship; she was laid up in 1942 and used as a floating oil depot under the number GR251. Of her sister vessels, Marcantonio Colonna was laid up in April 1942 and broken up in 1943; Des Geneys was also laid up in the same month and converted to a hull for charging batteries; and Vittorio Pisani was laid up in March 1947.

SPECIFICATIONS

COUNTRY: Italy
LAUNCH DATE: 24 March 1928
CREW: 48
DISPLACEMENT: surfaced 894 tonnes (880 tons); submerged 1075 tonnes (1058 tons)
DIMENSIONS: 68.2m x 6m x 4.9m (223ft 9in x 19ft 8in x 16ft 2in)
ARMAMENT: six 533mm (21in) torpedo tubes; one 120mm (4in) gun
POWERPLANT: twin screws, diesel/electric motors
RANGE: 9260km (5000nm) at 8 knots
PERFORMANCE: surfaced 15 knots; submerged 8.2 knots

Giuseppe Finzi

The *Giuseppe Finzi* was one of four boats of the Calvi class, whose class leader, *Pietro Calvi*, enjoyed considerable success against Allied convoys in the Atlantic before being scuttled after a violent battle with the sloop HMS *Lulworth* and other warships on 15 July 1942. Most Italian submarines in the Atlantic operated in the Azores area. *Giuseppi Finzi* was one of the first Italian submarines to be deployed to the Atlantic, but it was not until 1942 that she began to register some sinkings. At this time she was commanded by Cdr Giudice and was operating in the South Atlantic as part of the Da Vinci group of submarines (*Finzi*, *Torelli*, *Tazzoli* and *Morosini*), which was probably the most successful in the Italian Navy. On 9 September 1943, she was captured by the Germans at Bordeaux and numbered *UIT21*; she was scuttled on 25 August 1944.

SPECIFICATIONS

COUNTRY: Italy
LAUNCH DATE: 29 June 1935
CREW: 77
DISPLACEMENT: surfaced 1574 tonnes (1550 tons); submerged 2093 tonnes (2060 tons)
DIMENSIONS: 98.3m x 9.1m x 5.3m (322ft 4in x 29ft 10in x 17ft 4in)
ARMAMENT: eight 533mm (21in) torpedo tubes; two 120mm (4.7in) guns
POWERPLANT: twin screw, diesel/electric motors
RANGE: 24,817km (13,400nm) at 8 knots
PERFORMANCE: surfaced 16.8 knots; submerged 4.7 knots

Glauco (1905)

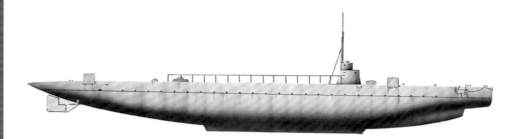

Built at the Venice Naval Dockyard to designs by Engineer Lurenti, *Glauco* belonged to the first mass-produced group of submarines built for the Italian Navy. When *Glauco* was laid down in 1903, petrol engines were still being fitted to submarines in spite of the volatile nature of the fuel they used, which led to numerous accidents. *Glauco*'s engines developed 600hp, giving a surface range of 1710km (922nm) at eight knots. Submerged, her electric motors developed 447kW (170hp) and range was 65km (35nm) at 5 knots. There were some differences between the boats, for example, *Glauco* had three torpedo tubes, but this was reduced to two in the rest. During the war these boats were employed for harbour defence at Brindisi and Venice. *Glauco* was removed from the effective list in 1916, having been used for training for some time.

SPECIFICATIONS

COUNTRY: Italy
LAUNCH DATE: July 1905
CREW: 30
DISPLACEMENT: surfaced 160 tonnes (157 tons); submerged 243 tons (240 tons)
DIMENSIONS: 36.8m x 4.3m x 2.6m (120ft 9in x 14ft 1in x 8ft 6in)
ARMAMENT: three 450mm (17.7in) torpedo tubes
POWERPLANT: twin screws, petrol engines, electric motors
RANGE: 1710km (922nm) at 8 knots
PERFORMANCE: surfaced 14 knots; submerged 7 knots

Glauco (1935)

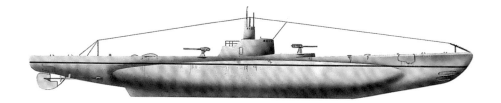

Glauco and her sister boat *Otaria* were originally ordered for the Portuguese Navy under the names *Delfim* and *Espadarte*, so they were completed for service in the Italian Navy. *Glauco*'s first war station in June 1940 was off the Algerian coast and in September she was transferred to the Atlantic, her very long range making her well suited for operations in that theatre. On 27 June 1941, *Glauco* was scuttled west of Gibraltar after having been damaged by gunfire from the destroyer HMS *Wishart*. Her sister boat, *Otaria*, was used to transport fuel and supplies to Axis forces in Tunisia early in 1943, this being at a time when Allied air power and naval forces combined were wreaking terrible havoc on Axis supply convoys in transit across the Mediterranean. *Glauco* survived the war and was discarded in 1948.

SPECIFICATIONS

COUNTRY: Italy
LAUNCH DATE: 5 January 1935
CREW: 59
DISPLACEMENT: surfaced 1071 tonnes (1055 tons); submerged 1346 tonnes (1325 tons)
DIMENSIONS: 73m x 7.2m x 5m (239ft 6in x 23ft 8in x 16ft 6in)
ARMAMENT: eight 533mm (21in) torpedo tubes; two 100mm (3.9in) guns
POWERPLANT: twin screws, diesel/electric motors
RANGE: 10,000km (5390nm) at 8 knots
PERFORMANCE: surfaced 17.3 knots; submerged 8.6 knots

Goubet I

At the end of the nineteenth century, the United Kingdom was considered France's main enemy, and, since British industry was stronger, the French tried to build up a navy of small but numerous coastal combatants such as torpedo boats and submarines.The greatest difficulty facing early submarine designers was to find an acceptable form of underwater propulsion. Steam power and compressed air were being tested, but they had limitations. An answer appeared in 1859 when Plante invented the lead accumulator. By 1880, this had been improved by coating the surface with red lead. At long last, the submarine designers had access to a power source that no longer relied on oxygen to function. *Goubet I* had a pointed, cylindrical hull with an observation dome. She was one of the first successful submarines, but was discarded because of her small size.

SPECIFICATIONS

COUNTRY: France
LAUNCH DATE: 1887
CREW: 2
DISPLACEMENT: surfaced 1.6 tonnes (1.57 tons); submerged 1.8 tonnes (1.77 tons)
DIMENSIONS: 5m x 1.7m x 1m (16ft 5in x 5ft 10in x 3ft 3in)
ARMAMENT: none
POWERPLANT: single-screw, electric motor
RANGE: not known
PERFORMANCE: surfaced 5 knots; submerged not known

Goubet II

Goubet II was laid down one year after the launch of *Goubet I*. Motive power was provided by a 4hp Siemens electric road car engine, and range at full speed was about 38km, or just over 20 nautical miles. Motive power was derived from a battery of Laurent-Cely accumulators carried in the lower portion of the hull. After a series of trials, *Goubet II*, like her predecessor, was rejected because of her small size. However, she was a well-planned, successful craft and the valuable experience gained during her building and trials was put to good use by later submarine designers. The acceptable solution to the propulsion problem – a combination of diesel engines for surface travel, and electric motors for use submerged – was not far away. It would take the Germans, however, to realize its full potential.

SPECIFICATIONS

COUNTRY: France
LAUNCH DATE: 1889
CREW: 2
DISPLACEMENT: surfaced 4.5 tonnes (4.42 tons); submerged 5 tonnes (4.9 tons)
DIMENSIONS: 8m x 1.8m x 1.8m (26ft 3in x 5ft 11in x 5ft 11in)
ARMAMENT: none
POWERPLANT: single screw, electric motor
RANGE: 38km (20.5nm) at full speed
PERFORMANCE: surfaced 6 knots; submerged not known

Grayling

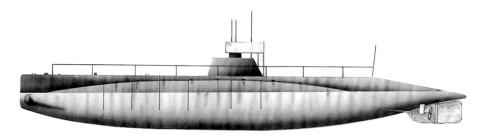

Grayling was formerly numbered *D2*, and later became *S18*. She was one of the last submarines in the US Navy to have petrol engines, which were a source of constant anxiety to her 15-man crew. *Grayling*'s engines developed 447kW (600hp), giving her a surface range of 2356km (1270nm) at cruising speed. The three boats of this D class began service off the East coast. All American submarines were named after fish; during World War II, so many new boats were built that the Navy ran out of existing fish names, so they invented names that in the future could be given to fish of newly-discovered species. When America entered the war, over half the submarines in commission were of World War I vintage. It was a telling indictment of US Naval policy during the interwar years, and it resulted in needless losses in the early months of the Pacific War.

SPECIFICATIONS

COUNTRY: United States
LAUNCH DATE: June 1909
CREW: 15
DISPLACEMENT: surfaced 292 tonnes (288 tons); submerged 342 tonnes (337 tons)
DIMENSIONS: 41m x 4.2m x 3.6m (134ft 6in x 13ft 9in x 11ft 11in)
ARMAMENT: four 457mm (18in) torpedo tubes
POWERPLANT: twin screws, two petrol engines, two electric motors
RANGE: 2356km (1270nm) at 10 knots
PERFORMANCE: surfaced 12 knots; submerged 9.5 knots

Guglielmo Marconi

Guglielmo Marconi was lead vessel of a class of six submarines, all but one of which were lost during World War II. (The exception was the *Luigi Torelli*, which was captured by the Japanese at Singapore when the news of Italy's armistice with the Allies broke, and ended the war immobilized at Kobe). *Marconi* was transferred to the Atlantic in the closing months of 1940 and, under Cdr Chialamberto, scored her first success in November when she sank a merchantman – already disabled by air attack – in the central Atlantic. She was lost in November 1941; the cause was never fully established, but one theory is that she was sunk in error by the German submarine *U67* (under Lt Cdr Mäller-Stïckheim), which was operating in the area at the time and which had registered some sinkings of British vessels.

SPECIFICATIONS

COUNTRY: Italy
LAUNCH DATE: 30 July 1939
CREW: 56
DISPLACEMENT: surfaced 1214 tonnes (1195 tons); submerged 1513 tonnes (1490 tons)
DIMENSIONS: 76.5m x 6.8m x 4.7m (251ft x 22ft 4in x 15ft 5in)
ARMAMENT: eight 533mm (21in) torpedo tubes; one 100mm (3.9in) gun
POWERPLANT: twin screw, diesel/electric motors
RANGE: 19,950km (10,750nm) at 8 knots
PERFORMANCE: surfaced 18 knots; submerged 8.2 knots

Gustave Zédé

Gustave Zédé was one of the last
steam-driven submarines built for
the French Navy and, at the time of her
completion in October 1914, she was one
of the fastest submarines in the world.
Her two reciprocating engines developed
1640hp, and her electric motors produced
1640hp. Her sister ship, Néréide, was
fitted with the originally specified diesel
motors which were only half as powerfulas
first envisaged. Gustave Zédé's underwater
range was 256km (138nm) at 5 knots. In
1921–22 the boat was fitted with diesel
engines taken from the former German
submarine U165. At the same time
Gustave Zédé was fitted with a new bridge,
and her fuel capacity was increased as
two ballast tanks were converted to carry
diesel fuel. She served in the Adriatic
during World War I, and was stricken from
the Navy List in 1937.

SPECIFICATIONS

COUNTRY: France
LAUNCH DATE: May 1913
CREW: 32
DISPLACEMENT: surfaced 862 tonnes (849 tons);
submerged 1115 tonnes (1098 tons)
DIMENSIONS: 74m x 6m x 3.7m (242ft 9in x 19ft 8in
x 12ft 2in)
ARMAMENT: eight 450mm (17.7in) torpedo tubes
POWERPLANT: twin screws, reciprocating engines,
electric motors
RANGE: 2660km (1433nm) at 10 knots
PERFORMANCE: surfaced 9.2 knots; submerged 6.5
knots

Gymnôte

Dupuy de Lôme, whose name was to become celebrated in the field of maritime design and engineering, prepared the initial drawings for *Gymnôte*, but after his death, the plans were revised by Gustave Zédé, who produced a single-hull steel submarine with a detachable lead keel. Electric power was provided by 204 cells spread along the lower part of the hull. Ordered in 1886, *Gymnôte* made over 2000 dives in all. She sank in dock at Toulon in 1907, was raised, and was scrapped in the following year. *Gymnôte* and *Gustave Zédé* were the last French submersibles to depend on electric motive power alone. They had proved the concept of its use, but they had also proved that it did not provide the whole of the answer. From now on, thinking would turn increasingly to a combination of diesel and electric power.

SPECIFICATIONS

COUNTRY: France
LAUNCH DATE: September 1888
CREW: 5
DISPLACEMENT: surfaced 30 tonnes (29.5 tons); submerged 31 tonnes (30.5 tons)
DIMENSIONS: 7.3m x 1.8m x 1.6m (58ft 5in x 5ft 11in x 5ft 6in)
ARMAMENT: two 355mm (14in) torpedo tubes
POWERPLANT: single-screw, electric motor
RANGE: not known
PERFORMANCE: surfaced 7.3 knots; submerged 4.2 knots

H. L. Hunley

H. *L. Hunley* was the first true submersible craft to be used successfully against an enemy. The main part of the hull was shaped from a cylindrical steam boiler, with the tapered ends added. Armament was a spar torpedo, an explosive charge on the end of a pole. The craft had a nine-man crew, eight to turn the handcranked propeller and one to steer. On 17 February 1864, commanded by Lt George Dixon, she slipped into Charleston Harbor and sank the newly commissioned Union corvette *Housatonic*, but was dragged down by the wave caused by the explosion of the torpedo. Years later, when the wreck was located on the sea bed, the skeletons of eight of the crew were discovered, still seated at their crankshaft. Named after her inventor, *H. L. Hunley* was one of a number of small submersibles built for the Confederate Navy.

SPECIFICATIONS

COUNTRY: Confederate States of America
LAUNCH DATE: 1863
CREW: 9
DISPLACEMENT: surfaced 2 tonnes/2 tons approx; submerged not known
DIMENSIONS: 12m x 1m x 1.2m (39ft 5in x 3ft 6in x 3ft 11in)
ARMAMENT: one spar torpedo
POWERPLANT: single screw, hand-cranked
RANGE: not known
PERFORMANCE: surfaced 2.5 knots; submerged not known

H1

H1 was one of eight Italian submarines that were exact copies of the British H class, and were all built by the Canadian Vickers Company, Montreal. She and her sisters were unique in that their electric motors developed more power than their diesels. One of the class, *H5*, was sunk in error by the British submarine *HB1* in the South Adriatic on 16 April 1918. All the H-class boats went on to serve in the early stages of World War II, and formed a submarine group that patrolled the Gulf of Genoa in the days after Italy's entry into the war in June 1940. *H1* was armed with a 76mm (3in) gun in 1941, shortly before she was withdrawn from first-line service. The boats served generally on training duties in home waters. *H31* was lost, cause unknown, in the Bay of Biscay, and *H49* was sunk off the Dutch coast. *H1* was scrapped in 1947.

SPECIFICATIONS

COUNTRY: Italy
LAUNCH DATE: 16 October 1916
CREW: 27
DISPLACEMENT: surfaced 370 tonnes (365 tons); submerged 481 tonnes (474 tons)
DIMENSIONS: 45.8m x 4.6m x 3.7m (150ft 3in x 15ft 4in x 12ft 5in)
ARMAMENT: four 450mm (17in) torpedo tubes
POWERPLANT: twin screws, diesel/electric motors
RANGE: not known
PERFORMANCE: surfaced 12.5 knots; submerged 8.5 knots

H4

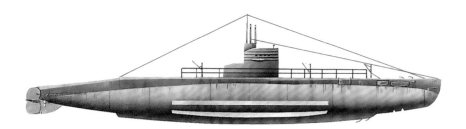

H4 was one of 17 boats ordered for the Imperial Russian Navy under the 1915 Emergency Programme. With the collapse of Tsarist Russia, a few were seized by the Bolsheviks and commissioned. Eleven were actually delivered to Russia in sections for assembly at the Baltic Shipyards. *H4*'s contract was cancelled, however, and she was purchased for the United States Navy from her builders, the Electric Boat Company, in 1918. The boats had been built to a Holland design, identical to the boats built for the United Kingdom, Italy and the US. In 1920, *H4* was renumbered *SS147*. The US H class had a designed depth limit of 6m (20ft) and, despite engine problems, were considered successful boats. *H4* was stricken in 1930 and broken up in 1931. This class should not be confused with the British and Chilean H class, also built by the Electric Boat Company.

SPECIFICATIONS
COUNTRY: United States
LAUNCH DATE: October 1918
CREW: 35
DISPLACEMENT: surfaced 398 tonnes (392 tons); submerged 529 tonnes (521 tons)
DIMENSIONS: 45.8m x 4.8m x 3.8m (150ft 3in x 15ft 9in x 12ft 6in)
ARMAMENT: four 457mm (18in) torpedo tubes
POWERPLANT: twin screws, diesel/electric motors
RANGE: 3800km (7041nm)
PERFORMANCE: surfaced 14 knots; submerged 10 knots

Hajen

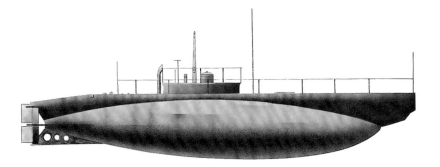

Hajen was the first submarine built for the Swedish Navy. She was designed by naval engineer Carl Richson, who had been sent to the US to study submarine development in 1900. *Hajen* was laid down at Stockholm in 1902. In 1916 she underwent a major rebuild, and her length was increased by 1.8m (6ft). She was withdrawn from service in 1922, and became a museum exhibit. Sweden, which for centuries had been a major power in Europe, had adopted a policy of neutrality in the 1860s, after which it made every effort to retain a strong defensive navy. With the odd exception, all its warships, including submarines, were Swedish-built. Sweden's shipbuilding industry had an important asset in that it had access to high-grade steel, thanks to the country's quality iron ore deposits.

SPECIFICATIONS

COUNTRY: Sweden
LAUNCH DATE: July 1904
CREW: 15
DISPLACEMENT: surfaced 108 tonnes (107 tons); submerged 130 tonnes (127 tons)
DIMENSIONS: 19.8m x 3.6m x 3m (64ft 11in x 11ft 10in x 9ft 10in)
ARMAMENT: one 457mm (18in) torpedo tube
POWERPLANT: single screw, paraffin engine, electric motor
RANGE: not known
PERFORMANCE: surfaced 9.5 knots; submerged 7 knots

Henri Poincaré

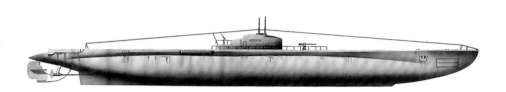

Built at Lorient, *Henri Poincaré* was one of 29 double-hulled ocean-going submarines of the Redoutable class laid down between 1925 and 1931. They were classified as ocean-going or first-class submarines, and were a considerable improvement over the preceding Requin class, but had their share of problems. *Prométhée*, was lost during trials on 8 July 1932, and another, *Phénix*, was lost in Indo-Chinese waters on 15 June 1939. *Henri Poincaré* was scuttled at Toulon in November 1942, along with her sister boats *Vengeur*, *Redoutable*, *Pascal*, *Achéron*, *L'Espoir* and *Fresnel*, but was salvaged by the Italians and returned to Genoa for overhaul. Designated *FR118*, she was sunk in September 1943 after being seized by German forces. France's Vichy-controlled submarines would have proved a valuable asset to the Allies, had they been released to the Free French.

SPECIFICATIONS

COUNTRY: France
LAUNCH DATE: 10 April 1929
CREW: 61
DISPLACEMENT: surfaced 1595 tonnes (1570 tons); submerged 2117 tonnes (2084 tons)
DIMENSIONS: 92.3m x 8.2m x 4.7m (302ft 10in x 26ft 11in x 15ft 5in)
ARMAMENT: nine 550mm (21.7in) and two 400mm (15.7in) torpedo tubes; one 82mm (3.2in) gun
POWERPLANT: twin screws, diesel/electric motors
RANGE: 18,530km (10,000nm) at 10 knots
PERFORMANCE: surfaced 17–20 knots; submerged 10 knots

Holland No. 1

Although the Irish-American inventor John P. Holland had produced some experimental submarine designs, including the *Fenian Ram*, the *Holland No. 1* was his first success. The diminutive craft was originally designed to be handcranked like previous submarines, but with the introduction of the newly-developed Brayton 4hp petrol engine, Holland was able to produce a more reliable vessel. *Holland No. 1* was built at the Albany Iron Works and was completed in 1878. After successful trials, the engine was removed and she was scuttled in 4.2m (14ft) of water on the Upper Passaic River. Years later she was raised, and she is now housed in the Paterson Museum, US. Holland's far-sighted faith in the petrol engine proved premature, other submarine designs of this period being still dependent on steam for their motive power.

SPECIFICATIONS

COUNTRY: United States
LAUNCH DATE: 1878
CREW: not known
DISPLACEMENT: surfaced 2.2 tonnes (2.16 tons); submerged not known
DIMENSIONS: 4.4m x 0.9m (14ft 6in x 2ft 11in)
ARMAMENT: none
POWERPLANT: single screw, petrol engine
RANGE: sot known
PERFORMANCE: surfaced not known; submerged not known

Holland VI

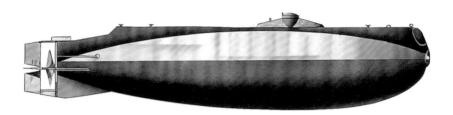

Holland VI was the first modern American submarine, and later became the prototype for British and Japanese submarines which combined petrol engine and battery power with hydroplanes. *Holland VI* entered service with the US Navy as the Holland in 1900. Her petrol engine developed 34kW (45hp) and her electric motor 56kW (75hp) when submerged. Diving depth was 22.8m (75ft). She served as a training boat until 1905, was re-numbered *SS1*, and scrapped in 1913. Although the American press praised the little Holland submarine and bestowed such lurid descriptions as 'Monster War Fish' on her, she was in fact a very primitive craft. She might not have been built at all, had Holland's political friends not persuaded the Navy to allocate funds to the venture. There was a very strong and influential Irish-American lobby in Congress at this time.

SPECIFICATIONS

COUNTRY: United States
LAUNCH DATE: May 1897
CREW: 7
DISPLACEMENT: surfaced 64 tonnes (63 tons); submerged 76 tonnes (74 tons)
DIMENSIONS: 16.3m x 3.1m x 3.5m (53ft 3in x 10ft 3in x 11ft 6in)
ARMAMENT: one 457mm (18in) torpedo tube; one pneumatic gun
POWERPLANT: single screw, petrol engine/electric motor
RANGE: submerged: 74km (40nm) at 3 knots
PERFORMANCE: surfaced 8 knots; submerged 5 knots

Hvalen

Hvalen was the only large submarine to be constructed for Sweden by a foreign power. She was bought from the Italian firm of Fiat-San Giorgio so that the Swedes might have the opportunity to evaluate a leading European design, and she made headline news with her epic 7600km (4096nm) voyage from Italy to Sweden unescorted. *Hvalen* was removed from the effective list in 1919 and was sunk as a target in 1924. The wreck was later raised and scrapped. Because of her neutral status, Sweden has always been regarded as something of a backwater in naval affairs, but the fact remains that her shipyards have produced some of the world's best and most effective warships, including submarines. The Swedish government always tried to be self-sufficient in military and naval matters, recognising the dangers of relying on foreign partners.

SPECIFICATIONS

COUNTRY: Sweden
LAUNCH DATE: 1909
CREW: 30
DISPLACEMENT: surfaced 189 tonnes (186 tons); submerged 233 tonnes (230 tons)
DIMENSIONS: 42.4m x 4.3m x 2.1m (139ft 1in x 14ft 1in x 6ft 11in)
ARMAMENT: two 457mm (18in) torpedo tubes
POWERPLANT: single screw, petrol engines/electric motors
RANGE: 8338km (4500nm) at 10 knots
PERFORMANCE: surfaced 14.8 knots; submerged 6.3 knots

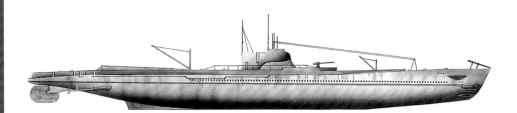

At the time of their construction, *I7* and her sister boat, *I8*, were the largest submarines built for the Japanese Navy. They were intended for the scouting role, and carried a reconnaissance seaplane. They could stay away from base for 60-day periods, cruising for over 14,000nm at 16 knots, and could dive to a depth of 99m (325ft). Between them, the two boats sank seven Allied merchant ships totalling 42,574 (41,902 tons). *I7* was sunk by the American destroyer *Monaghan* on 22 June 1943. *I8* was modified to carry four Kaiten suicide submarines in place of her aircraft hangar. She was sunk by the destroyers USS *Morrison* and *Stockton* on 30 March 1945 while attempting to attack American ships involved in the Okinawa landings. Many Japanese warships were lost in suicide attacks during this campaign.

SPECIFICATIONS

COUNTRY: Japan
LAUNCH DATE: 3 July 1935
CREW: 100
DISPLACEMENT: surfaced 2565 tonnes (2525 tons); submerged 3640 tonnes (3583 tons)
DIMENSIONS: 109.3m x 9m x 5.2m (358ft 7in x 29ft 6in x 17ft)
ARMAMENT: six 533mm (21in) torpedo tubes, one 140mm (5.5in) gun
POWERPLANT: twin screws, diesel/electric motors
RANGE: 26,600km (14,337nm) at 16 knots
PERFORMANCE: surfaced 23 knots; submerged 8 knots

I15

The I15-class submarines were highly specialized scouting boats, with streamlined hulls and conning towers. Compared with earlier classes of scouting submarines, the seaplane hangar was also streamlined, being a smooth, rounded fairing that extended forward as part of the conning tower. Although designed to mount four 25mm (1in) AA guns, they were completed with a single twin 25mm (1in) mounting. During World War II, some vessels had their hangar and catapult removed and replaced by a second 140mm (5.5in) gun, being reclassed as attack submarines. Only one boat of the fairly large class, *I36*, survived the war, being surrendered at Kobe. *I15* (under Cdr Ishikawa) was lost on 2 November 1942. As the war progressed and the Americans recaptured the Pacific islands the Japanese submarine fleet was penned into its home bases, its radius of action reduced.

SPECIFICATIONS

COUNTRY: Japan
LAUNCH DATE: 1939
CREW: 100
DISPLACEMENT: surfaced 2625 tonnes (2584 tons); submerged 3713 tonnes (3654 tons)
DIMENSIONS: 102.5m x 9.3m x 5.1m (336ft 3in x 30ft 6in x 16ft 9in)
ARMAMENT: six 533mm (21in) torpedo tubes; one 140mm (5.5in) and two 25mm (1in) AA guns
POWERPLANT: two shafts, diesel/electric motors
RANGE: 45,189km (24,400nm) at 10 knots
PERFORMANCE: surfaced 23.5 knots; submerged 8 knots

I21

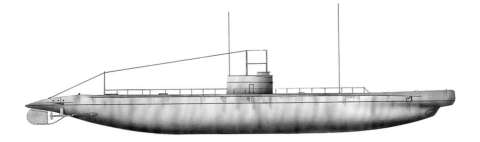

One of two vessels that were Japan's first ocean-going submarines, *I21* was built from Italian plans of the Fiat-Laurenti F1 type. She was built at the Kawasaki yard in Kobe and completed in 1920. Her number was changed to *RO2* in 1924, and she was stricken in 1930. In the meantime, the *I21* number had been re-allocated to a new submarine, launched in March 1926. The design of this vessel was based on the German submarine *UB125*, which had been given to Japan after surrendering in 1918. The new *I21* was leader of a class of four boats, all of which went on to see service in the Pacific War. In 1939 they received new designations, *I21* becoming *I121* and so on. *I21/I121* was scrapped; the others were lost in action. Very few Japanese submarines survived until the final surrender.

SPECIFICATIONS

COUNTRY: Japan
LAUNCH DATE: November 1919
CREW: 45
DISPLACEMENT: surfaced 728 tonnes (717 tons); submerged 1063 tonnes (1047 tons)
DIMENSIONS: 65.6m x 6m x 4.2m (215ft 3in x 19ft 8in x 13ft 9in)
ARMAMENT: five 457mm (18in) torpedo tubes
POWERPLANT: two screws, diesel/electric motors
RANGE: 19,456km (10,500nm) at 8 knots
PERFORMANCE: surfaced 13 knots; submerged 8 knots

Intelligent Whale

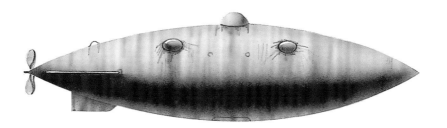

Intelligent Whale was the first submarine constructed for the Union Navy, and was built in response to Confederate vessels of the same type; for example the *David* (so named because it was seen as a giant-killer), which was steam-propelled and was really more of a semi-submersible torpedo boat than a true submarine. Thirteen men were carried in the *Whale*, six of them propelling the cylindrical cigar-shaped hull by hand, and the remainder intended to leave the vessel by a trap door in the floor in order to secure mines to the hulls of enemy vessels. After several tests, the project was finally abandoned in 1872 and *Intelligent Whale* was put on display at the Washington Navy Yard. In general, Confederate attempts to produce workable submersibles were more effective than those of their Federal opponents.

SPECIFICATIONS

COUNTRY: United States
LAUNCH DATE: 1862
CREW: 13
DISPLACEMENT: surfaced not known; submerged not known
DIMENSIONS: 9.4m x 2.6m x 2.6m (30ft 10in x 8ft 6in x 8ft 6in)
ARMAMENT: mines
POWERPLANT: single screw, hand-cranked
RANGE: not known
PERFORMANCE: surfaced 4 knots; submerged 4 knots

Isaac Peral

Isaac Peral was Spain's first major submarine. She was built by the Fore River Company in the United States and modelled on the Holland design. She attained 15.36 knots on the surface during trials. Surface range was 5386km (2903 nautical miles) at 11 knots; range submerged was 130km (70nm) at full power from her 358kW (480hp) electric motors. She was renumbered O1 in 1930, later being reduced to a hulk and numbered AO. Her single 76mm (3in) gun was fixed to a collapsible mount, and was not a permanent feature. Spain did not maintain a substantial submarine force; after General Franco's victory in the Civil War, boats were obtained from Italy. The Civil War created an enormous drain on Spain's resources, one of the reasons why Franco chose to remain neutral in World War II.

SPECIFICATIONS

COUNTRY: Spain
LAUNCH DATE: July 1916
CREW: 35
DISPLACEMENT: surfaced 499 tonnes (491 tons); submerged 762 tonnes (750 tons)
DIMENSIONS: 60m x 5.8m x 3.4m (196ft 10in x 19ft x 11ft 2in)
ARMAMENT: four 457mm (18in) torpedo tubes, one 76mm (3in) gun
POWERPLANT: twin screws, diesel/electric motors
RANGE: 5386km (2903nm) at 11 knots
PERFORMANCE: surfaced 15 knots; submerged 8 knots

J1

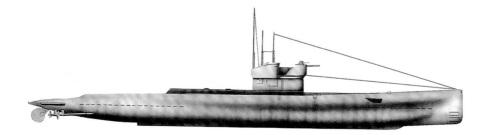

J1 was built in response to a perceived threat from German submarines then entering service and reputed to be capable of 22 knots. As first completed, *J1*'s large forward free-flooding tank brought the bows down in the water, causing loss of speed when surfaced. Later the bows were raised, curing this pitching tendency, and the submarine was then able to maintain 17 knots surfaced in heavy seas. Range at 12.5 knots surfaced was 9500km (5120nm). Later, a 102mm (4in) gun was positioned high up at the front of the conning tower in place of the 76mm (3in) weapon. On 5 November 1916, *J1* torpedoed and damaged the German battleships *Grosser-Kurfurst* and *Kronprinz*. *J1* was handed over to Australia in 1919, and was broken up in 1924. Only seven J-class boats were built, one of which was lost accidentally.

SPECIFICATIONS

COUNTRY: United Kingdom
LAUNCH DATE: November 1915
CREW: 44
DISPLACEMENT: surfaced 1223 tonnes (1204 tons); submerged 1849 tonnes (1820 tons)
DIMENSIONS: 84m x 7m x 4.3m (275ft 7in x 22ft 11in x 14ft 1in)
ARMAMENT: six 457mm (18in) torpedo tubes; one 76mm (3in) gun
POWERPLANT: triple screws, diesel/electric motors
RANGE: 9500km (5120nm) at 12.5 knots
PERFORMANCE: surfaced 17 knots; submerged 9.5 knots

K

K4

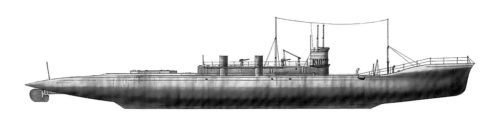

I n 1915, the British Admiralty decided to design a class of exceptionally fast ocean-going submarines that could keep up with the battlefleet. As diesel engines of the period could not develop adequate power to sustain a surface speed of 24 knots, steam turbines were used instead, with electric motors for underwater operation. The turbine machinery took up nearly 40 per cent of a K boat's length, and had to be shut down when she was submerged, with large lids covering the funnel uptakes. The boats were a disaster, no fewer than five of the 17 built prior to 1919 being lost in accidents. It was hardly surprising that morale in the Submarine Flotillas to which the K boats were assigned was not at its highest level. In general, the K boats were relegated to anti-submarine patrols. *K4* was accidentally rammed and sunk by *K6* in February 1918.

SPECIFICATIONS

COUNTRY: United Kingdom
LAUNCH DATE: 15 July 1916
CREW: 50–60
DISPLACEMENT: surfaced 2174 tonnes (2140 tons); submerged 2814 tonnes (2770 tons)
DIMENSIONS: 100.6m x 8.1m x 5.2m (330ft 1in x 26ft 7in x 17ft 1in)
ARMAMENT: ten 533mm (21in) torpedo tubes; three 102mm (4in) guns
POWERPLANT: twin screws, steam turbines/electric motors
RANGE: 5556km (3000nm) at 13.5 knots
PERFORMANCE: surfaced 23 knots; submerged 9 knots

K26

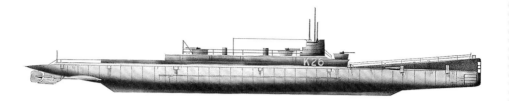

K *26* was the only one of the notorious K boats to be built after 1919, being completed in 1919 and scrapped in 1931. One K-boat incident might have cost the future King George VI his life. He was a passenger on board *K3* when the boat was being put through her paces. The submarine's commander prepared to dive but, instead of gently nosing under the surface, the boat went down at a steep angle, hit the sea bead and stuck fast, with her bows buried deep in mud. The water was about 46m (150ft) deep, so a sizeable portion of the boat was still protruding above the surface, her propellers still turning. Luckily she was released without damage after about 20 minutes of frantic effort. Other K-boat crews were not so lucky. None of the boats was destroyed in action; all five losses were caused by accidents.

SPECIFICATIONS

COUNTRY: United Kingdom
LAUNCH DATE: August 1919
CREW: 50–60
DISPLACEMENT: surfaced 2174 tonnes (2140 tons); submerged 2814 tonnes (2770 tons)
DIMENSIONS: 100.6m x 8.1m x 5.2m (330ft 1in x 26ft 7in x 17ft 1in)
ARMAMENT: ten 533mm (21in) torpedo tubes; three 102mm (4in) guns
POWERPLANT: twin screws, steam turbines/electric motors
RANGE: 5556km (3000nm) at 13.5 knots
PERFORMANCE: surfaced 23 knots; submerged 9 knots

L3 (1915)

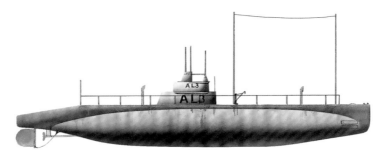

L3 was the first American submarine to be fitted with a deck gun. This retracted vertically into a deckhouse until only a small portion of the barrel was left exposed, so reducing underwater drag. The United States ended World War I with about 120 submarines, although by this time the US had lost their submarine design lead (established in the early years of the 20th century by John Holland) to the European naval powers. At this time, America's best submarines were roughly comparable with Britain's H and L classes. Very little progress in submarine design was made in the US during the interwar years, and it took the threat of another war to act as the spur that would once again bring her to the forefront. US ocean-going submarines soon achieved superiority in the Pacific.

SPECIFICATIONS

COUNTRY: United States
LAUNCH DATE: February 1915
CREW: 35
DISPLACEMENT: surfaced 457 tonnes (450 tons); submerged 556 tonnes (548 tons)
DIMENSIONS: 51m x 5.3m x 4m (167ft 4in x 17ft 4in x 13ft 1in)
ARMAMENT: four 457mm (18in) torpedo tubes; one 76mm (3in) gun
POWERPLANT: twin screws, diesel/electric motors
RANGE: 6270km (3380nm) at 11 knots
PERFORMANCE: surfaced 14 knots; submerged 8 knots

L3 (1931)

L*3* was one of a large class of Russian submarines. On the night of 16 April 1943, commanded by Capt 3rd Class Konovalov, she intercepted a German convoy of eight ships evacuating refugees from the Hela peninsula in the Baltic to the west, and sank the large steamship *Goya*. Of the 6385 persons on board, only 165 were rescued. It was the climax of a long and successful operational career that began with minelaying operations in the Baltic in June 1941, days after the German invasion of Russia. Russian submarine operations in the Baltic were a considerable threat to German supply and reinforcement traffic. Minelaying continued to be *L3*'s principal occupation, and she did not register her first success until August 1942, when she sank the 5580-tonne (5492-ton) steamer *C.F. Liljevalch*. *L3* served for several years after the war, and was scrapped in 1959.

SPECIFICATIONS

COUNTRY: Russia
LAUNCH DATE: July 1931
CREW: 50
DISPLACEMENT: surfaced 1219 tonnes (1200 tons); submerged 1574 tonnes (1550 tons)
DIMENSIONS: 81m x 7.5m x 4.8m (265ft 9in x 24ft 7in x 15ft 9in)
ARMAMENT: six 533mm (21in) torpedo tubes; one 100mm (3.9in) gun
POWERPLANT: twin screws, diesel/electric motors
RANGE: 11,112km (6000nm) at 9 knots
PERFORMANCE: surfaced 15 knots; submerged 9 knots

L10

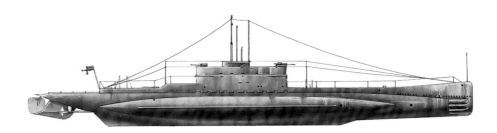

After the Battle of Jutland in May 1916, German surface forces rarely put to sea, and targets for Allied submarines were few and far between. Then, in April 1918, the German High Seas Fleet once more ventured out in strength to attack convoys between Britain and Scandinavia, and these activities continued – albeit on a reduced scale – until almost the end of the war, with destroyers the main participants. During one of these sorties, on 3 October 1918, the British submarine *L10* intercepted the German destroyer *S33* and sank her, only to be sunk herself by other enemy warships. During these last weeks of the war the German destroyers were very active, and British submarines often became the hunted rather than the hunters. It was an indication of what determined surface forces could do in the anti-submarine war.

SPECIFICATIONS

COUNTRY: United Kingdom
LAUNCH DATE: 24 January 1918
CREW: 36
DISPLACEMENT: surfaced 904 tonnes (890 tons); submerged 1097 tonnes (1080 tons)
DIMENSIONS: 72.7m x 7.2m x 3.4m (238ft 6in x 23ft 8in x 11ft 2in)
ARMAMENT: four 533mm (21in) torpedo tubes; one 102mm (4in) gun
POWERPLANT: twin screws, diesel/electric motors
RANGE: 7038km (3800nm) at 10 knots
PERFORMANCE: surfaced 17.5 knots; submerged 10.5 knots

L23

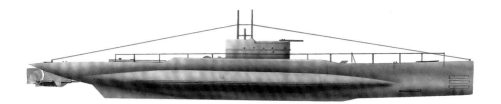

L23 was one of the last surviving units of the large L class of submarines, 17 of which were built after the end of World War I. One of the L-class boats, L12, torpedoed and sank the German submarine UB90 on 16 October 1918, while the enemy boat was recharging her batteries on the surface of the North Sea at night. The second boat of the class, L2, was subjected to a fierce gunfire and depth charge attack by American warships escorting a convoy in February 1918, one shell scoring a direct hit on the pressure hull just behind the conning tower as the boat re-surfaced. Fortunately, the Americans realized their mistake in time to avert a tragedy. Three boats, L23, L26 and L27, served on training duties in World War II; L23 foundered under tow off Nova Scotia en route to the breaker's yard in May 1946.

SPECIFICATIONS

COUNTRY: United Kingdom
LAUNCH DATE: 1 July 1919
CREW: 36
DISPLACEMENT: surfaced 904 tonnes (890 tons); submerged 1097 tonnes (1080 tons)
DIMENSIONS: 72.7m x 7.2m x 3.4m (238ft 6in x 23ft 8in x 11ft 2in)
ARMAMENT: four 533mm (21in) torpedo tubes; one 102mm (4in) gun
POWERPLANT: twin screws, diesel/electric motors
RANGE: 8338km (4500nm)
PERFORMANCE: surfaced 17.5 knots; submerged 10.5 knots

Luigi Settembrini

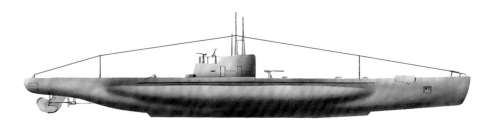

L uigi Settembrini was a fast, short-range, partial double-hull boat with excellent manoeuvrability. Until 1940, she served in the Red Sea. Fron 1940 to 1943 she alternated combat patrols (on which she proved completely ineffective) and supply runs to North Africa with periods of service at the Italian Navy's Submarine School. After Italy joined the Allies, the boat was used for training until she was accidentally rammed and sunk by the US escort destroyer Framet. Settembrini's sister boat, Ruggiero Settimo, followed much the same operational career; she was launched in March 1931, completed in April 1932, and was eventually stricken from the Navy list on 23 March 1947. Very few of the wartime Italian submarines were judged effective enough to continue in a combat role in the post-war years.

SPECIFICATIONS
COUNTRY: Italy
LAUNCH DATE: 28 September 1930
CREW: 56
DISPLACEMENT: surfaced 968 tonnes (953 tons); submerged 1171 tonnes (1153 tons)
DIMENSIONS: 69m x 6.6m x 4.4m (226ft 8in x 21ft 8in x 14ft 5in)
ARMAMENT: eight 533mm (21in) torpedo tubes; one 102mm (4in) gun
POWERPLANT: twin screws, diesel/electric motors
RANGE: 16,668km (9000nm) at 8 knots
PERFORMANCE: surfaced 17 knots; submerged 7.5 knots

M1

In 1917, the British Admiralty suspended construction work on four K boats and revised their plans, to turn them into submarine monitors, known as the M class, by mounting a single 305mm (12in) gun in the front part of an extended conning tower. The gun could be fired from periscope depth within 30 seconds of a target being sighted, or in 20 seconds if the submarine was surfaced. The snag was that the gun could not be reloaded under water, so the submarine had to surface after each round was fired; which earned the M class the nickname 'Dip Chicks'. The M boats were intended to be the equivalent of Germany's 'cruiser submarines'. They were never used operationally; three were completed and two lost in accidents, the *M1* herself being lost in November 1925 when she collided with the freighter *Vidar*.

SPECIFICATIONS

COUNTRY: United Kingdom
LAUNCH DATE: 9 September 1917
CREW: 60–70
DISPLACEMENT: surfaced 1619 tonnes (1594 tons); submerged 1977 tonnes (1946 tons)
DIMENSIONS: 90m x 7.5m x 4.9m (295ft 7in x 24ft 7in x 16ft 1in)
ARMAMENT: four 533mm (21in) torpedo tubes; one 305mm (12in) gun
POWERPLANT: twin screws, diesel/electric motors
RANGE: 7112km (3840nm) at 10 knots
PERFORMANCE: surfaced 15 knots; submerged 9 knots

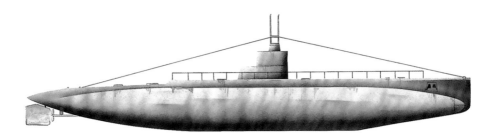

W hen the US entered World War I in 1917, there were around 50 submarines in service with the US Navy. These ranged from the small A and B boats in the Philippines to the more advanced boats of the L class. The seven units of the N class were slightly smaller than the previous L class, and had reduced engine power in order to achieve greater engine reliability. This led to the adoption of more moderate power in the subsequent O, R and S classes, the last of which were launched in 1922. *N1* and her class were the first US submarines to have metal bridges, and the last until 1946 to be designed without deck guns. *N1*, renumbered *SS53* in 1920, was broken up in 1931. The US Navy's submarines were used mainly in the coastal defence role in World War I, as a result of their restricted endurance.

SPECIFICATIONS

COUNTRY: United States
LAUNCH DATE: December 1916
CREW: 35
DISPLACEMENT: surfaced 353 tonnes (348 tons); submerged 420 tonnes (414 tons)
DIMENSIONS: 45m x 4.8m x 3.8m (147ft 4in x 15ft 9in x 12ft 6in
ARMAMENT: four 457mm (18in) torpedo tubes
POWERPLANT: twin screws, diesel/electric motors
RANGE: submerged 6485km (3500nm) at 5 knots
PERFORMANCE: surfaced 13 knots; submerged 11 knots

Nautilus (1800)

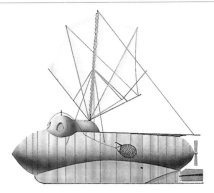

Nautilus was designed by Robert Fulton. Having no success with his project in America, Fulton went to France in 1797, where his plans for Nautilus were accepted. She was to become the first submarine to be built to a government contract. Her hull comprised an iron framework covered with copper sheets, and buoyancy was controlled by hand pumps. Nautilus was propelled by a sail when on the surface, and by hand-cranked propeller when submerged. During trials in Le Havre harbour, Nautilus remained under water at a depth of 7.6m (25ft) for one hour. A detachable explosive charge was secured just above the conning tower, ready to be fastened to the hull of an enemy vessel. After the French lost interest in the project, Fulton took his design to Britain, but despite the fact that Nautilus was consistently successful during trials, she was not adopted.

SPECIFICATIONS
COUNTRY: United States
LAUNCH DATE: 1800
CREW: 3
DISPLACEMENT: surfaced 19 tonnes(18.69 tons); submerged not known
DIMENSIONS: 6.4m x 1.2m (21ft x 3ft 7in)
ARMAMENT: single detachable explosive charge
POWERPLANT: single screw, hand-cranked
RANGE: sot known
PERFORMANCE: not known

Nautilus (1914)

Nautilus was built in response to a request from the British Admiralty for a 1016-tonne (1000-ton) submarine with a surface speed of 20 knots. The idea was that such a craft could accompany units of the fleet and, if necessary, act in a protective role. However, calculations showed that the best speed that could be achieved was 17 knots, and that on a displacement of 1290 tonnes (1270 tons). Vickers, the designers, approached Fiat, but the latter firm could not guarantee the required 1380kW (1850hp) from their new 12-cylinder diesel engines. Nevertheless, *Nautilus* was laid down in 1913 and the big diesel engines were installed. She never entered operational service, but was stationed at Portsmouth as a depot ship. This apparent failure conceals the fact that *Nautilus* was a giant step forward, not only in size but in power. She was scrapped in 1922.

SPECIFICATIONS

COUNTRY: United Kingdom
LAUNCH DATE: December 1914
CREW: 35
DISPLACEMENT: surfaced 1464 tonnes (1441 tons); submerged not available
DIMENSIONS: 78.8m x 7.9m x 5.4m (258ft 6in x 25ft 11in x 17ft 9in)
ARMAMENT: eight 457mm (18in) torpedo tubes
POWERPLANT: twin screws, diesel/electric motors
RANGE: 9816km (5300nm) at 11 knots
PERFORMANCE: surfaced 17 knots; submerged 10 knots

Nautilus (1930)

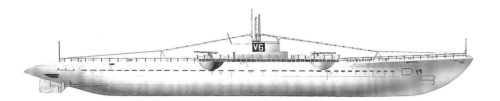

The USS *Nautilus* (*SS168*, formerly *V6*) was one of three V-class boats designed as long-endurance ocean-going vessels with a heavy armament, the others being Argonaut and Narwhal. In 1940 she was re-fitted to carry 5104 litres (19,320 gal) of aviation fuel for long-range seaplanes. In June 1942, she was one of a force of submarines patrolling north-west of Midway Island to counter an anticipated Japanese invasion force, and in August, together with *Argonaut*, she landed US raiders on Makin, in the Gilbert Islands. In October 1942, she sank two freighters off the east coast of Japan. Together with *Narwhal*, she acted as a marker submarine in Operation *Landcrab*, the reconquest of Attu in the North Pacific. In March 1944, she sank another large freighter off the Mandate Islands. She was scrapped in 1945.

SPECIFICATIONS

COUNTRY: United States
LAUNCH DATE: 15 March 1930
CREW: 90
DISPLACEMENT: surfaced 2773 tonnes (2730 tons); submerged 3962 tonnes (3900 tons)
DIMENSIONS: 113m x 10m x 4.8m (370ft 8in x 33ft 3in x 15ft 9in)
ARMAMENT: six 533mm torpedo tubes, two 152mm (6in) guns
POWERPLANT: twin screws, diesel/electric motors
RANGE: 33,336km (18,000nm) at 10 knots
PERFORMANCE: surfaced 17 knots; submerged 8 knots

Nereide

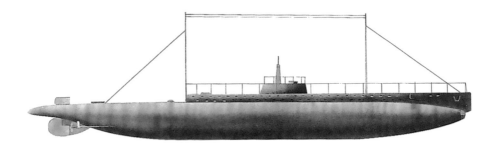

Nereide and her sister *Nautilus* were the first submarines designed by Engineer Bernardi, later to become renowned as a submarine designer. Both were laid down on 1 August 1911 and completed in 1913. *Nereide*'s smooth, sleek hull shape was similar to that of a torpedo boat, and her two torpedo tubes were mounted in the bow. A third, deck-mounted torpedo tube was originally planned, but never fitted. *Nereide* was sunk on 5 August 1915 near Pelagosa Island in the Adriatic, by torpedoes from the Austrian submarine *U5*. Apart from a few loaned by Germany, Austria's submarines were built in the country's own yards, and were very compact boats. The majority of Italian submarines designed around this period were efficient, capable boats, and were well suited to the waters of the Adriatic, their principal operating area.

SPECIFICATIONS

COUNTRY: Italy
LAUNCH DATE: July 1913
CREW: 35
DISPLACEMENT: surfaced 228 tonnes (225 tons); submerged 325 tonnes (320 tons)
DIMENSIONS: 40m x 4.3m x 2.8m (134ft 2in x 14ft 1in x 9ft 2in)
ARMAMENT: two 450mm (17in) torpedo tubes
POWERPLANT: twin screws, diesel/electric motors
RANGE: 7412km (4000nm) at 10 knots
PERFORMANCE: surfaced 13.2 knots; submerged 8 knots

Nordenfelt

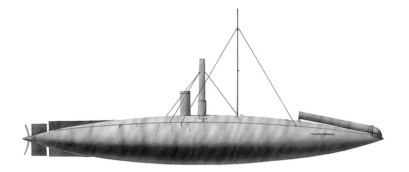

Nordenfelt was British-designed and built at Landskrona in Sweden. Laid down in 1882, she was one of the world's first steam-powered submarines. Her hull was almost circular in section, with frames spaced 0.6m (2ft) apart along its length. Diving depth was 15m (50ft). Most of her interior was taken up with the machinery, boilers and a steam accumulator, which had a heat exchanger at the bottom. Steam from the boiler was conveyed through the coils of the heater, giving up its latent heat to the water in the accumulator, which was then returned to the boiler via a feed pump. By this means, a large amount of superheated water could be stored in the pear-shaped tank. When this was released into the main boiler at a lower pressure, it turned into steam. The engine was fired in harbour, and took three days to heat up the reservoir fully.

SPECIFICATIONS

COUNTRY: Greece
LAUNCH DATE: 1885
CREW: not known
DISPLACEMENT: surfaced 61 tonnes (60 tons); submerged not known
DIMENSIONS: 19.5m x 2.7m (64ft x 8ft 10in)
ARMAMENT: one 355mm (14in) gun; one 25.4mm (1in) gun (fitted later)
POWERPLANT: single screw, compound engine
RANGE: not known
PERFORMANCE: surfaced 9 knots; submerged 4 knots

Nymphe

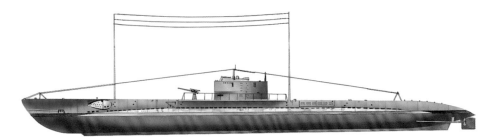

On the outbreak of World War II, the group of medium-range submarines to which *Nymphe* belonged was the largest class of such vessels in the French Navy, and they operated intensively until the French collapse in June 1940. French submarines were equally useful on the surface or submerged. *Nymphe* was one of a batch of four boats built by Ateliers Loire-Simonot; they were laid down in 1923 and completed in 1927. In spite of having a complex torpedo layout, involving a double revolving mounting, *Nymphe* and her consorts were successful ships. Three of the batch were scuttled at Toulon on 27 November 1942, shortly before the harbour was occupied by troops of the II SS-Panzer Corps, this action following the Allied landings in North Africa earlier in the month. *Nymphe* herself was scrapped in 1938.

SPECIFICATIONS

COUNTRY: France
LAUNCH DATE: 01 April 1926
CREW: 41
DISPLACEMENT: surfaced 619 tonnes (609 tons); submerged 769 tonnes (757 tons)
DIMENSIONS: 64m x 5.2m x 4.3m (210ft x 17ft 1in x 14ft 1in)
ARMAMENT: seven 551mm (21.7in) torpedo tubes; one 76mm (3in) gun
POWERPLANT: twin-screw diesel/electric motors
RANGE: 6485km (3500nm) at 7.5 knots
PERFORMANCE: surfaced 13.5 knots; submerged 7.5 knots

Oberon

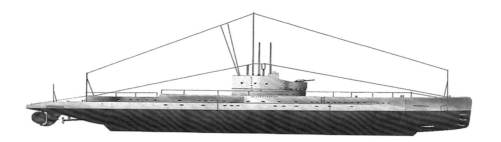

HMS *Oberon* was an ocean-going saddle-tank boat developed from the L-type minelaying submarines of World War I. She was laid down in 1924 and completed in 1927. Originally designated *O1*, the boat was of an advanced design and had a very respectable radius of action, which made the O class ideal for service in Far Eastern waters. Of the first three boats, however, only *Oxley* got that far, serving with the Royal Australian Navy from 1927 to 1931 before returning to home waters, where she was lost on 10 September 1939 after being rammed in error by HMS *Triton*. A second group of six O-class boats was built in 1928–29, four of these serving in the East Indies before being transferred to the Mediterranean in 1940. Only two of this batch survived the war. *Oberon* was scrapped at Rosyth in August 1945.

SPECIFICATIONS

COUNTRY: United Kingdom
LAUNCH DATE: 24 September 1926
CREW: 54
DISPLACEMENT: surfaced 1513 tonnes (1490 tons); submerged 1922 tonnes (1892 tons)
DIMENSIONS: 83.4m x 8.3m x 4.6m (273ft 8in x 27ft 3in x 15ft 1in)
ARMAMENT: eight 533mm (21in) torpedo tubes
POWERPLANT: twin screws, diesel/electric motors
RANGE: 9500km (5633nm) at 10 knots
PERFORMANCE: surfaced 13.7 knots; submerged 7.5 knots

O Class

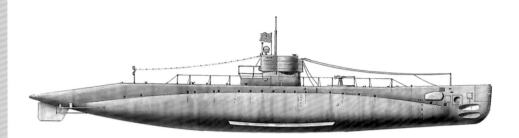

The 16 O-class submarines were all built for the US Navy in 1917–18. Only one, *O7*, saw active service in World War I, carrying out war patrols off the eastern seaboard of the United States from July 1918. Of the others, *O11*, *O13*, *O14*, *O15* and *O16* were broken up in 1930; *O2*, *O3*, *O4*, *O6*, *O7*, *O8* and *O10* were broken up in 1946. *O5* sank on 28 October 1923; *O9* went missing on 20 June 1941; *O1* was stricken in 1938. One of the boats, *O12*, was sold to Norway in 1930, renamed *Nautilus* and used in an abortive attempt to reach the North Pole. She was broken up in 1931. During their service lives most of the O-class boats were used for training. They had a designed diving depth of 61m (200ft). Because of their restricted endurance, American submarines were generally confined to coastal patrol duties in World War I.

SPECIFICATIONS

COUNTRY: United States
LAUNCH DATE: 9 July 1918 (*O1*)
CREW: 29
DISPLACEMENT: surfaced 529 tonnes (521 tons); submerged 639 tonnes (629 tons)
DIMENSIONS: 52.5m x 5.5m x 4.4m (172ft 3in x 18ft 1in x 14ft 5in)
ARMAMENT: four 457mm (18in) torpedo tubes; one 76mm (3in) gun
POWERPLANT: two shafts, diesel/electric motors
RANGE: 10,191km (5500nm) at 11.5 knots
PERFORMANCE: surfaced 14 knots; submerged 10.5 knots

Odin

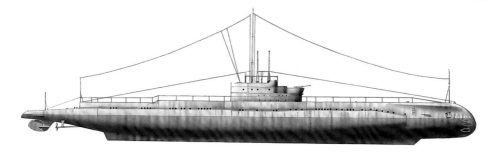

O*din* was the lead boat of the second batch of O class submarines built in the late 1920s. The O class boats had a fairly heavy armament, but at the expense of handling quality. Together with *Olympus*, *Orpheus* and *Otus*, she served in the East Indies and then went to the Mediterranean in 1940, joining other O class boats already there. On 14 June 1940 – only four days after Italy's entry into the war and while operating out of Malta – she was sunk in the Gulf of Taranto by the Italian destroyer *Strale*. Her sister boat *Orpheus* was sunk off Tobruk by the destroyer *Turbine* two days later. *Oswald* was sunk by the destroyer *Vivaldi* south of Calabria on 1 August 1940, and *Olympus* was mined off Malta on 8 May 1942. The other two boats, *Osiris* and *Otus*, were scrapped at Durban in September 1946.

SPECIFICATIONS

COUNTRY: United Kingdom
LAUNCH DATE: 5 May 1928
CREW: 54
DISPLACEMENT: surfaced 1513 tonnes (1490 tons); submerged 1922 tonnes (1892 tons)
DIMENSIONS: 83.4m x 8.3m x 4.6m (273ft 8in x 27ft 3in x 15ft)
ARMAMENT: eight 533mm (21in) torpedo tubes
POWERPLANT: twin screws, diesel/electric motors
RANGE: 9500km (5633nm) at 10 knots
PERFORMANCE: surfaced 17.5 knots; submerged 8 knots

Orzel

Orzel was ordered in January 1935 and was funded by public subscription. She was a large, ocean-going boat with excellent all-round qualities and was Dutch-built, together with her sister ship *Wilk* (*Wolf*). Diving depth was 80m (200ft) and submerged range was 190km (102nm) at five knots. *Orzel* was commissioned in February 1939. On 14 September 1939, the Polish submarines were ordered to break out from the Baltic and make for British ports; *Wilk* arrived on 20 September and *Orzel* (under Lt Cdr Grudzinski) on 14 October via Reval, after an adventurous voyage without charts. On 8 April 1940 *Orzel* sank two large troop transports at the start of the German invasion of Norway, but was lost in a mine barrage off the Norwegian coast on 8 June. Her sister, *Wilk*, attacked and sank a Dutch submarine in error on 20 June 1940.

SPECIFICATIONS

COUNTRY: Poland
LAUNCH DATE: 1938
CREW: 56
DISPLACEMENT: surfaced 1117 tonnes (1100 tons); submerged 1496 tonnes (1473 tons)
DIMENSIONS: 84m x 6.7m x 4m (275ft 7in x 22ft x 13ft 1in)
ARMAMENT: 12 550mm (21.7in) torpedo tubes, one 105mm (4in) gun
POWERPLANT: twin screws, diesel/electric motors
RANGE: 13,300km (7169nm) at 10 knots
PERFORMANCE: surfaced 15 knots; submerged 8 knots

Parthian

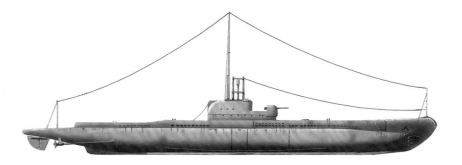

The six vessels in the Parthian class were laid down in 1928 and completed in 1930–31. All were fitted with Vulcan clutches and high capacity batteries. The 14 torpedoes carried were Mk VIIIs, standard armament on all subsequent British submarines of that period. During World War II, the surviving boats of the Parthian class had a 20mm (0.79in) Oerlikon added and could take 18 M2 mines, laid from the torpedo tubes, in place of torpedoes. All were originally deployed in Chinese waters, but transferred to the Mediterranean in 1940. *Parthian* went missing in the Adriatic on 11 August 1943, presumed mined; *Perseus* was torpedoed by the Italian submarine *Enrico Toti* off Zante; *Phoenix* was sunk by the Italian torpedo-boat *Albatros* off Sicily; and *Pandora* was bombed by Italian aircraft at Malta. Only *Proteus* survived, becoming a training vessel.

SPECIFICATIONS

COUNTRY: United Kingdom
LAUNCH DATE: 22 June 1929
CREW: 53
DISPLACEMENT: surfaced 1788 tonnes (1760 tons); submerged 2072 tonnes (2040 tons)
DIMENSIONS: 88.14m x 9.12m x 4.85m (289ft 2in x 29ft 11in x 15ft 11in)
ARMAMENT: eight 533mm (21in) torpedo tubes; one 102mm (4in) gun
POWERPLANT: two shafts, diesel/electric motors
RANGE: 9500km (5633nm) at 10 knots
PERFORMANCE: surfaced 17.5 knots; submerged 8.6 knots

Pietro Micca

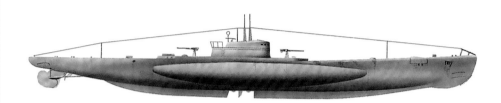

This was a long-range, torpedo and minelaying boat with a partial double hull and an operation depth of 90m (295ft). Although an experimental vessel, and not repeated, *Pietro Micca* was a good, manoeuvrable seaboat. Surfaced range at full speed was 4185km (2256nm). Her first war operation, on 12 June 1940, under Cdr Meneghini, was to lay a barrage of 40 mines off Alexandria; on 12 August she laid more mines in the same area, and unsuccessfully attacked a destroyer two days later. In February and March 1941, she ran supplies from Tobruk to the Italian garrison on the island of Leros, and in summer 1942 she joined other submarines in transporting fuel and supplies to ports in Cyrenaica. She continued to act as a transport submarine until her career came to an abrupt end on 29 July 1943 when she was sunk in the Straits of Otranto by HMS *Trooper*.

SPECIFICATIONS

COUNTRY: Italy
LAUNCH DATE: 31 March 1935
CREW: 72
DISPLACEMENT: surfaced 1595 tonnes (1570 tons); submerged 2000 tonnes (1970 tons)
DIMENSIONS: 90.3m x 7.7m x 5.3m (296ft 3in x 25ft 3in x 17ft 4in)
ARMAMENT: six 533mm (21in) torpedo tubes; two 120mm (4.7in) guns
POWERPLANT: twin screws, diesel/electric motors
RANGE: 10,300km (5552nm) at 9 knots
PERFORMANCE: surfaced 14.2 knots; submerged 7.3 knots

Pioneer

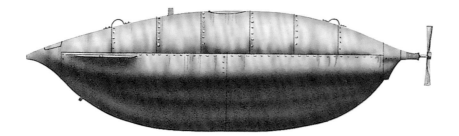

In the American Civil War, the Confederacy was especially interested in any development which promised to break the Union maritime blockade. This early submersible – the only privateer submarine ever built – was laid down in late 1861 at the government yard at New Basin in New Orleans. She had an oval-shaped hull, as did others that succeeded her. Operated by a three-man crew, two of whom worked the hand cranking system which drove the external single propeller; her only armament was a spar torpedo, a long shaft with explosive at the end which had to be rammed into the side of the target vessel. In March 1862, *Pioneer* was issued with a Letter of Marque, which licensed her to sink Union warships. Her crew would collect a bounty of 20 per cent of the estimated value of their victim. In 1952, *Pioneer* was moved to the Louisiana State Museum.

SPECIFICATIONS
COUNTRY: Confederate States of America
LAUNCH DATE: February 1862
CREW: 3
DISPLACEMENT: surfaced 4 tonnes (3.9 tons); submerged not known
DIMENSIONS: 10.3m x 1.2m x 1.2m (33ft 9in x 3ft 11in x 3ft 11in)
ARMAMENT: one spar torpedo
POWERPLANT: single screw, hand-cranked
RANGE: sot known
PERFORMANCE: surfaced not known; submerged not known

Porpoise

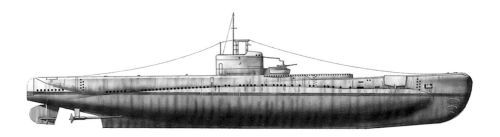

HMS *Porpoise* was leader of a class of six boats launched between 1932 and 1938. Three further boats were cancelled in 1941. The vessels of the class served in many different theatres from home waters to the West Indies, the Mediterranean, and the China Station. Five were lost in various ways, with *Rorqual*, deployed to the Eastern Fleet in 1944, the only one to survive the Second World War. *Grampus* was sunk by the Italian torpedo-boats *CI10* and *Circe* off Augusta on 24 June 1940; *Narwhal* went missing off Norway in July 1940; *Cachalot* was rammed by the Italian torpedo-boat *Papa* off Cyrenaica on 4 August 1941; *Seal* was damaged by a mine before surrendering to the Germans on 5 May 1940; and *Porpoise* herself was bombed and sunk by Japanese aircraft in the Malacca Strait on 19 January 1945.

SPECIFICATIONS

COUNTRY: United Kingdom
LAUNCH DATE: 30 August 1932
CREW: 61
DISPLACEMENT: surfaced 1524 tonnes (1500 tons); submerged 2086 tonnes (2053 tons)
DIMENSIONS: 81.5m x 9m x 13.75m (267ft 5in x 29ft 9in x 13ft 9in)
ARMAMENT: six 533mm (21in) torpedo tubes; one 102mm (4in) gun
POWERPLANT: twin screws, diesel/electric motors
RANGE: 10,191km (5500nm) at 10 knots
PERFORMANCE: surfaced 15 knots; submerged 8.75 knots

R1

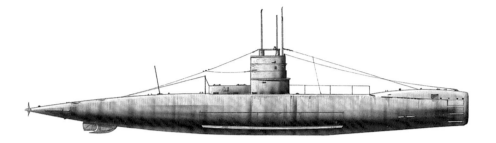

In 1917, the Royal Navy was struggling to counter the German U-boats' toll of British merchant shipping. The most significant development was the convoy system, but proposals for submarines able to hunt other submarines were also considered. *R1* was the forerunner of the modern ASW hunter-killer fleet submarine. Ten vessels were completed. They were intended to chase U-boats on the surface, and sink them with torpedoes. *R1* had a hull form similar to that of the earlier H class, and a pronounced bulge above the bow. She was highly streamlined, with internal ballast tanks and no gun. Five powerful hydrophones with bearing instruments were carried in the bow compartment. These vessels were a daring solution to a problem which nearly brought Britain to disaster, but they arrived too late to have any effect.

SPECIFICATIONS

COUNTRY: United Kingdom
LAUNCH DATE: April 1918
CREW: 36
DISPLACEMENT: surfaced 416 tonnes (410 tons); submerged 511 tonnes (503 tons)
DIMENSIONS: 49.9m x 4.6m x 3.5m (163ft 9in x 15ft 1in x 11ft 6in)
ARMAMENT: six 457mm (18in) torpedo tubes
POWERPLANT: single screw, diesel/electric 1200 hp motors
RANGE: 3800km (2048nm) at 8 knots
PERFORMANCE: surfaced 15 knots; submerged 9.5 knots

Reginaldo Giuliani

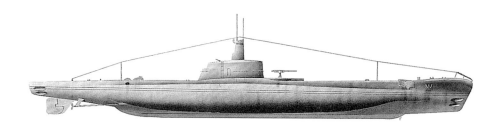

Reginaldo Giuliani and her three sisters of the Liuzzi class were developments of the Brin class. Maximum diving depth was 90m (290ft). In 1940, Giuliani was deployed to the French Atlantic ports for operations against British convoys; she was later converted to transport cargo to the Far East. Seized by the Japanese at Singapore after Italy's surrender, Giuliani was handed over to Germany as UIT23. On 14 February 1944, she was intercepted and sunk in the Malacca Straits by HMS Tally Ho (under Cdr Bennington). A sister ship, Alpino Bagnolini, also captured, and renumbered UIT22, was sunk by South African aircraft off the Cape of Good Hope on 11 March 1944; another, Capitano Tarantini, was sunk on 15 December 1940 by HMS Thunderbolt. Console Generale Liuzzo was scuttled off Crete after a battle with the destroyers HMS Defender, Dainty and Ilex.

SPECIFICATIONS

COUNTRY: Italy
LAUNCH DATE: 30 December 1939
CREW: 58
DISPLACEMENT: surfaced 1184 tonnes (1166 tons); submerged 1507 tonnes (1484 tons)
DIMENSIONS: 76.5m x 6.8m x 4.7m (251ft x 22ft 4in x 15ft 5in)
ARMAMENT: eight 533mm (21in) torpedo tubes; one 100mm (3.9in) gun
POWERPLANT: twin screw, diesel/electric motors
RANGE: 19,950km (10,750nm) at 8 knots
PERFORMANCE: surfaced 17.5 knots; submerged 8.4 knots

Requin

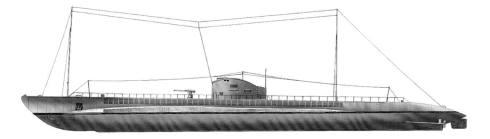

Laid down in 1923 and completed three years later, *Requin* (*Shark*) was leader of a class of nine submarines that were completely modernized in 1935–37. They had chequered fortunes during World War II. *Caiman* and *Marsouin* escaped from Algiers in November 1942, at the time of the Allied landings in North Africa and sailed to Toulon, where *Caiman* was scuttled. *Requin*, *Dauphin*, *Phoque* and *Espadon* were seized by the Germans at Bizerta in December 1942 but were never commissioned, being broken up later. *Morse* struck a mine and sank off Sfax on 10 June 1940; *Souffleur* was sunk by the British submarine *Parthian* (under Cdr Rimington) during the Syrian campaign on 29 June 1941; and *Narval* was sunk by a mine on 15 December 1940, en route for Malta, her captain having refused to return to Toulon after France's surrender.

SPECIFICATIONS

COUNTRY: France
LAUNCH DATE: 19 July 1924
CREW: 54
DISPLACEMENT: surfaced 974 tonnes (990 tons); submerged 1464 tonnes (1441 tons)
DIMENSIONS: 78.25m x 6.84m x 5.10m (256ft 7in x 22ft 6in x 16ft 9in)
ARMAMENT: ten 550mm (21.7in) torpedo tubes
POWERPLANT: twin screws, diesel/electric motors
RANGE: 10,469km (5650nm) at 10 knots
PERFORMANCE: surfaced 15 knots; submerged 9 knots

Resurgam II

Resurgam II was designed by George Garrett. She had a cigar-shaped hull with spindle ends, and was able to withstand a pressure of 32kg per square mm (71 pounds per square inch), enabling her to dive to a depth of about 45.5m (150ft). Propulsion was by steam on the Lamm fireless principle. A coal furnace heated water in a large steam boiler; the fire door and smoke-escape valve leading to a short funnel inside the superstructure were then closed. Latent heat turned the water into steam when the throttle valve was opened, thereby supplying the engine. Initial trials were promising, and Garrett decided to set up base on the Welsh coast. However, as Resurgam II was being towed to her new berth in February 1880, she sank during a storm. She still lies where she sank off the British coast, although there are plans to raise her.

SPECIFICATIONS

COUNTRY: United Kingdom
LAUNCH DATE: December 1879
CREW: 2
DISPLACEMENT: surfaced 30 tonnes (29.5 tons); submerged not known
DIMENSIONS: 13.7m x 2.1m (44ft 11in x 6ft 11in)
ARMAMENT: none
POWERPLANT: single screw, Lamm steam locomotive
RANGE: not known
PERFORMANCE: surfaced 3 knots; submerged not known

Rubis

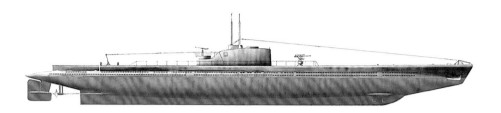

Rubis was one of six vessels of the Saphir class of minelaying submarine. Of all French submarines, these were arguably the best suited to their task. Their mines were stowed in wells in the outer ballast tanks and had direct release mechanism. In March 1940, *Rubis* joined the 10th Flotilla and the 2nd Submarine Division at Harwich, and began minelaying operations off Norway on 10 May, claiming eleven enemy freighters and the submarine-chaser *UJD*. The collapse of France in June 1940 found her in Dundee, and her crew elected to join the Free French forces, continuing to operate in the North Sea. In August 1941 she torpedoed a freighter off Norway. Minelaying later in the war claimed at least four more feighters, as well as the submarine chasers *UK1113*, *UJ1116* and *R402* on 21 December 1944, making her the most successful minelayer of the war.

SPECIFICATIONS

COUNTRY: France
LAUNCH DATE: 30 Sepember 1931
CREW: 42
DISPLACEMENT: surfaced 773 tonnes (761 tons); submerged 940 tonnes (925 tons)
DIMENSIONS: 65.9m x 7.12m x 4.3m (216ft 1in x 23ft 3in x 14ft 6in)
ARMAMENT: three 550mm (21.7in) and two 400mm (15.7in) torpedo tubes; one 75mm (3in) gun; 32 mines
POWERPLANT: twin screws, diesel/electric motors
RANGE: 12,971km (7000nm) at 7.5 knots
PERFORMANCE: surfaced 12 knots; submerged 9 knots

S1

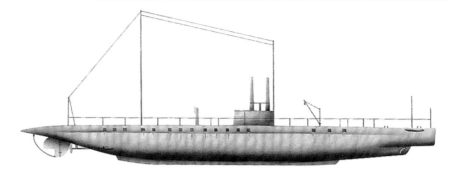

S *1* was based on the Italian Laurenti type, having a partial double hull with ten watertight compartments. Her diesel engines developed 485kW (650hp), the electric motors 298kW (400hp). Only three boats of the S class were completed. There were no fewer than 23 classes of submarine in service with the Royal Navy during World War I, of which by far the most numerous was the E class, with 58 boats. The C class came next, with 38, followed by the H1 class with 20, the K class with 17, the G class with 14, the A class with 13, the B class with 11 and the H21 and K classes with 10 each. The building of some classes continued after the war; 14 more H21s were built after 1919, as were 11 of the L9 class, which had eight boats in service during World War I. All three S-class boats, *S1*, *S2* and *S3*, were transferred to the Italian Navy in 1915, and were discarded in 1919.

SPECIFICATIONS

COUNTRY: United Kingdom
LAUNCH DATE: 28 February 1914
CREW: 31
DISPLACEMENT: surfaced 270 tonnes (265 tons); submerged 330 tonnes (324 tons)
DIMENSIONS: 45m x 4.4m x 3.2m (147ft 8in x 14ft 5in x 10ft 6in)
ARMAMENT: two 457mm (18in) torpedo tubes, one 12-pounder gun
POWERPLANT: twin screws, diesel/electric motors
RANGE: 2963km (1600nm) at 8.5 knots
PERFORMANCE: surfaced 13 knots; submerged 8.5 knots

S28

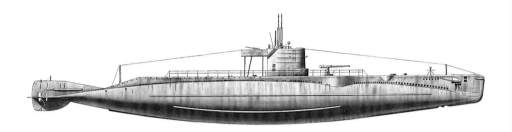

In December 1941, more than half US submarines belonged to the old O, R and S classes of World War I vintage. The so-called Old S class comprised four separate groups of 38 boats. In October 1943 *S28*, under Lt Cdr Sislet, sank a Japanese freighter in the Pacific, but no further successes were recorded before she herself was lost in July 1944, having failed to surface during a training exercise at Pearl Harbor. Some of the S class were transferred to the Royal Navy in 1942: *S1* became *P552*; *S21* became *P553*; *S22* became *P554*; *S24* became *P555*; *S25* became *P551* and then the Polish *Jastrzab*, and *S29* became *P556*. War losses among the remainder included *S26* (sunk in a collision on 24 January 1942), *S27* (ran aground on 19 June 1942), *S36* (ran aground on 20 January 1942), *S39* (ran aground on 14 August 1942), and *S44* (sunk by a Japanese destroyer on 7 October 1943).

SPECIFICATIONS

COUNTRY: United States
LAUNCH DATE: 20 September 1922
CREW: 42
DISPLACEMENT: surfaced 864 tonnes (850 tons); submerged 1107 tonnes (1090 tons)
DIMENSIONS: 64.3m x 6.25m x 4.6m (211ft x 20ft 6in x 15ft 3in)
ARMAMENT: four 533mm (21in) torpedo tubes; one 102mm (4in) gun
POWERPLANT: two-shaft diesels
RANGE: 6333km (3420nm) at 6.5 knots
PERFORMANCE: surfaced 14.5 knots; submerged 11 knots

Scire

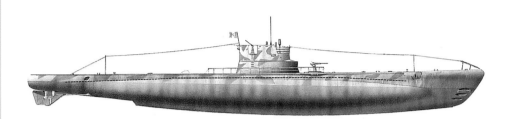

S *cire* was one of the Adua class of 17 short-range vessels. These had a double hull with blisters and were a repeat of the previous Perla class. They gave good service during World War II and, although their surface speed was low they were strong and very manoeuvrable. All except one (*Macalle*, which was in the Red Sea) operated in the Mediterranean. Only one boat, *Alagi*, survived World War II. *Scire* and another boat, *Gondar*, were modified in 1940–41 for the carriage of human torpedoes; these were known as *SLC*s (*Siluro a Lente Corsa*, or Slow Course Torpedoes) and nicknamed *Maiale* (Pig). Built or modified at San Bartolomeo torpedo workshop, they carried two men, an officer and a petty officer or seaman, and were used on a number of successful operations. *Scire* was sunk off Haifa, Palestine, on 10 August 1942 by the British armed trawler *Islay*.

SPECIFICATIONS

COUNTRY: Italy
LAUNCH DATE: 15 November 1936
CREW: 45
DISPLACEMENT: surfaced 691 tonnes (680 tons); submerged 880 tonnes (866 tons)
DIMENSIONS: 60.2m x 6.5m x 4.6m (197ft 6in x 21ft 4in x 15ft 1in)
ARMAMENT: six 530mm (21in) torpedo tubes, one 100mm (3.9in) gun
POWERPLANT: two diesel engines, two electric motors
RANGE: 9260km (5000nm) at 8 knots
PERFORMANCE: surfaced 14 knots; submerged 7 knots

Surcouf

The *Surcouf* was in effect an experimental, one-off boat, described by the French Navy as a 'Corsair submarine'. She was fitted with the largest calibre of guns permitted under the terms of the Washington Treaty and, at the outbreak of war, she was the largest, heaviest submarine in the world. She would remain so until the Japanese 400 series entered service in World War II. In June 1940, *Surcouf* escaped from Brest – where she was being refitted – and sailed for Plymouth, where she was seized by the Royal Navy (her crew resisting, with casualties on both sides). She was later turned over to the Free French Naval Forces, carried out patrols in the Atlantic and took part in the seizure of the islands of St Pierre and Miquelon off Newfoundland. The *Surcouf* was lost on 18 February 1942, in collision with an American freighter in the Gulf of Mexico.

SPECIFICATIONS

COUNTRY: France
LAUNCH DATE: 18 October 1929
CREW: 118
DISPLACEMENT: surfaced 3302 tonnes (3250 tons); submerged 4373 tonnes (4304 tons)
DIMENSIONS: 110m x 9.1m x 9.07m (360ft 10in x 29ft 9in x 29ft 9in)
ARMAMENT: two 203mm (8in) guns, eight 551mm (21.7in) and four 400mm (15.75in) torpedo tubes
POWERPLANT: twin screws, diesel/electric motors
RANGE: 18,530km (10,000nm) at 10 knots
PERFORMANCE: surfaced 18 knots; submerged 8.5 knots

Swordfish (1916)

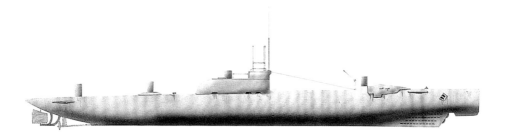

Just before the outbreak of World War I, the British Admiralty issued a requirement for a submarine capable of achieving 20 knots on the surface. The result was the diesel-powered *Nautilus* (launched in 1914), which produced very disappointing results. In spite of this, the Admiralty pressed ahead with plans for a 20-knot submarine. A 1912 proposal by the engineer Laurenti was re-examined and developed further by Scott. *Swordfish*'s small funnel was lowered electrically and the well covered by a plate. Closing down the funnel took a minute and a half, the heat inside the submarine proving bearable. *Swordfish* was the first submarine to have an experimental emergency telephone buoy fitted. In 1917, after a few months of trials work, *Swordfish* was converted into a surface patrol craft, and was broken up in 1922.

SPECIFICATIONS

COUNTRY: United Kingdom
LAUNCH DATE: 18 March 1916
CREW: 25
DISPLACEMENT: surfaced 947 tonnes (932 tons); submerged 1123 tonnes (1105 tons)
DIMENSIONS: 70.5m x 7m x 4.5m (231ft 4in x 23ft x 14ft 9in)
ARMAMENT: two 533mm (21in) and four 457mm (18in) torpedo tubes
POWERPLANT: twin screws, impulse reaction turbines
RANGE: 5556km (3000nm) at 8.5 knots
PERFORMANCE: surfaced 18 knots; submerged 10 knots

Swordfish (1931)

This was the second boat in the first group of S class submarines. Of the twelve in the group, only four survived World War II. *Swordfish* disappeared without trace off Ushant on or about 10 November 1940, possibly sunk by a mine. Of the other boats, *Seahorse* and *Starfish* were sunk by German minesweepers in the Heligoland Bight; *Shark* was sunk by German minesweepers off Skudesnes in Norway; *Salmon* was mined southwest of Norway; *Snapper* was lost in the Bay of Biscay (cause unknown); *Spearfish* was torpedoed by *U34* off Norway; *Sunfish* was bombed in error by British aircraft while on passage to North Russia (she was to have been assigned to the Soviet Navy as the *B1*); and *Sterlet* was sunk by German trawlers in the Skagerrak. The class leader, *Sturgeon*, served in the Royal Netherlands Navy (1943–45) as the Zeehond.

SPECIFICATIONS

COUNTRY: United Kingdom
LAUNCH DATE: 10 November 1931
CREW: 38
DISPLACEMENT: surfaced 650 tonnes (640 tons); submerged 942 tonnes (927 tons)
DIMENSIONS: 58.8m x 7.3m x 3.2m (192ft 11in x 23ft 11in x 10ft 6in)
ARMAMENT: six 533mm (21in) torpedo tubes; one 76mm (3in) gun
POWERPLANT: twin shafts, diesel/electric motors
RANGE: 7412km (4000nm) at 10 knots
PERFORMANCE: surfaced 15 knots; submerged 10 knots

Thames

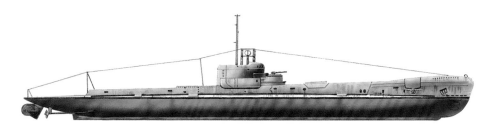

Designed with a high surface speed for Fleet work, *Thames* and her sisters, *Severn* and *Clyde*, were built by Vickers-Armstrong at Barrow-in-Furness. The outbreak of World War II found *Thames* serving with the 2nd Submarine Flotilla, and in the winter of 1939–40 she joined other boats of the flotilla (*Oberon*, *Triton*, *Triumph*, *Thistle*, *Triad*, *Trident* and *Truant*) in operations against enemy shipping off Norway. On 23 July 1940, *Thames* was sunk by a mine in the Norwegian Sea. *Severn* and *Clyde* served in home waters until 1941, when they deployed to the Mediterranean. On 20 June 1940, *Clyde* (under Lt Cdr Ingram) obtained a torpedo hit on the bows of the German battlecruiser *Gneisenau* off Trondheim. Both boats sank a respectable tonnage of enemy ships. In 1944, they deployed to the Eastern Fleet. *Severn* was scrapped at Bombay and *Clyde* at Durban in 1946.

SPECIFICATIONS

COUNTRY: United Kingdom
LAUNCH DATE: 26 January 1932
CREW: 61
DISPLACEMENT: surfaced 1834 tonnes (1805 tons); submerged 2680 tonnes (2723 tons)
DIMENSIONS: 99.1m x 8.5m x 4.1m (325ft 2in x 27ft 11in x 13ft 6in)
ARMAMENT: eight 533mm (21in) torpedo tubes; one 100mm (4in) gun
POWERPLANT: two shafts, diesel/electric motors
RANGE: 9265km (5000nm) at 10 knots
PERFORMANCE: surfaced 21.75 knots; submerged 10 knots

Thistle

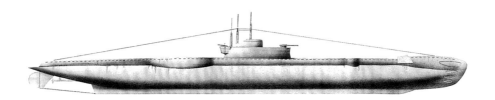

Thistle was one of 22 submarines of the T-class (first group), the first of which – *Triton* – was launched in October 1937 and the last – *Trooper* – in March 1942. Most saw active service in the Mediterranean. No fewer than fourteen of this group were lost between September 1939 and October 1943; *Thistle* herself was sunk off Norway by the *U4* on 10 April 1940. Of the remainder, *Triton* was sunk in the Adriatic by the Italian *TB Clio*; *Thunderbolt* (formerly *Thetis*) was sunk by the corvette *Cicogna* off Sicily; *Tarpon* was sunk in the North Sea by the German minesweeper *M6*; *Triumph*, *Tigris*, *Triad*, *Talisman*, *Tetrarch*, *Traveller* and *Trooper* were all lost through unknown causes in the Mediterranean; *Tempest* was sunk by the *TB Circe* in the Gulf of Taranto; *Thorn* by the *TB Pegaso* off Tobruk; and *Turbulent* by Italian *MTBs* off Sardinia.

SPECIFICATIONS

COUNTRY: United Kingdom
LAUNCH DATE: 25 October 1938
CREW: 59
DISPLACEMENT: surfaced 1107 tonnes (1090 tons); submerged 1600 tonnes (1575 tons)
DIMENSIONS: 80.8m x 8m x 4.5m (265ft 1in x 26ft 6in x 14ft 9in)
ARMAMENT: ten 533mm (21in) torpedo tubes; one 100mm (4in) gun
POWERPLANT: twin screws, diesel/electric motors
RANGE: 7041km (3800nm) at 10 knots
PERFORMANCE: surfaced 15.25 knots; submerged 9 knots

Turtle

Although not a true submersible, all of *Turtle* was under the surface when she was in action except for a tiny conning tower fitted with glass ports so that the occupant could find his way to the target. She was built by David Bushnell, who, during the American War of Independence, had carried out experiments with floating tide-borne mines. He subsequently decided to built a manned semi-submersible craft that could transport an explosive charge to the hull of an enemy ship. The charge was carried outside the hull, and was attached to the target by an auger that was drilled into the hull of the enemy vessel. A clockwork timing device gave *Turtle* time to escape. In September 1776, an American soldier, Ezra Lee, tried to attach an explosive charge to HMS *Eagle* in the Hudson River, but the auger broke. It was the first-ever underwater war mission.

SPECIFICATIONS

COUNTRY: United States
LAUNCH DATE: 1776
CREW: 1
DISPLACEMENT: surfaced 2 tonnes (1.96 tons); submerged 2 tonnes (1.96 tons)
DIMENSIONS: 1.8m x 1.3m (5ft 11in x 4ft 6in)
ARMAMENT: one 68kg (150lb) detachable explosive charge
POWERPLANT: single screw, hand-cranked
RANGE: not known
PERFORMANCE: surfaced not known; submerged not known

U class (1937)

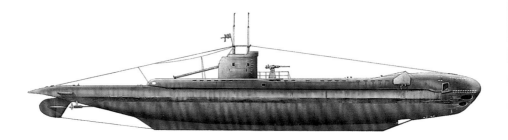

The U class submarines, 51 boats in all, were built on two groups by Vickers-Armstrong, either at Barrow-in-Furness or on the Tyne. All boats served in home waters and the Mediterranean during World War II, except for five boats which went to the East Indies for ASW training and four which were loaned to the RCN for the same purpose. The boats, which were small and manoeuvrable, proved very effective in the confined waters of the Mediterranean and the Aegean, but war losses were high. *Undine*, *Unity*, *Umpire* and *Uredd* (*RNN*) were lost in home waters; *Unbeaten* in the Bay of Biscay; and *Undaunted*, *Union*, *Unique*, *Upholder*, *Urge*, *Usk*, *Usurper* and *Utmost* in the Mediterranean, together with the unnamed U-class boats *P32*, *P33*, *P38* and *P48*. Another boat, *Untamed*, was lost on trials.

SPECIFICATIONS

COUNTRY: United Kingdom
LAUNCH DATE: 5 October 1937 (HMS *Undine*, class leader)
CREW: 31
DISPLACEMENT: surfaced 554 tonnes (545 tons); submerged 752 tonnes (740 tons)
DIMENSIONS: 54.9m x 4.8m x 3.8m (180ft 1in x 15ft 9in x 12ft 9in)
ARMAMENT: four 533mm (21in) torpedo tubes; one 76mm (3in) gun
POWERPLANT: twin screws, diesel/electric motors
RANGE: 7041km (3800nm) at 10 knots
PERFORMANCE: surfaced 11.2 knot; submerged 10 knots

U1

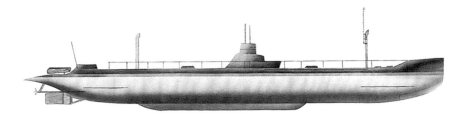

Strangely enough, the German Naval Staff at the turn of the century failed to appreciate the potential of the submarine, and the first submarines built in Germany were three Karp-class vessels ordered by the Imperial Russian Navy in 1904. Germany's first practical submarine, *U1*, was not completed until 1906. She was, however, one of the most successful and reliable of the period. Her two kerosene engines developed 400hp, as did her electric motors. *U1* had an underwater range of 80km (43nm). Commissioned in December 1906, she was used for experimental and training purposes. In February 1919, she was stricken, sold and refitted as a museum exhibit by her builders, Germaniawerft of Kiel. She was damaged by bombing in World War II, but subsequently restored. Double hulls and twin screws were used from the first in German U-boats.

SPECIFICATIONS

COUNTRY: Germany
LAUNCH DATE: 04 August 1906
CREW: 22
DISPLACEMENT: surfaced 554 tonnes (545 tons); submerged 752 tonnes (740 tons)
DIMENSIONS: 54.9m x 4.8m x 3.8m (180ft 1in x 15ft 9in x 12ft 9in)
ARMAMENT: four 533mm (21in) torpedo tubes; one 76mm (3in) gun
POWERPLANT: twin screws, diesel/electric motors
RANGE: 7041km (3800nm) at 10 knots
PERFORMANCE: surfaced 11.2 knot; submerged 10 knots

U2

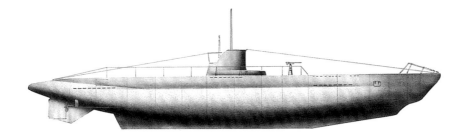

Under the terms of the Versailles Treaty, Germany was forbidden to build submarines, but during the 1920s she set up clandestine design teams in Spain, Holland and Russia. The first boat was built for Finland in 1927 and this was the prototype for *U2*, one of the first Type II submarines intended for coastal service. The diesel engines developed 261kW (350hp), and the electric motors developed 134kW (180hp). The early Type IIs were all used for training, and some of the most talented and successful of Germany's submarine commanders in World War II learned their trade in them. In March 1940, *U2* joined other German U-boats in an unsuccessful 'hunter-killer' operation against British and French submarines in the North Sea. On 8 April 1944, *U2* was lost in a collision west of Pillau during a training sortie in the Baltic.

SPECIFICATIONS

COUNTRY: Germany
LAUNCH DATE: July 1935
CREW: 25
DISPLACEMENT: surfaced 254 tonnes (250 tons); submerged 302 tonnes (298 tons)
DIMENSIONS: 40.9m x 4.1m x 3.8m (133ft 2in x 13ft 5in x 12ft 6in)
ARMAMENT: three 533mm (21in) torpedo tubes, one 20mm (0.8in) AA gun
POWERPLANT: twin screws, diesel/electric motors
RANGE: 1688km (912nm) at 10 knots
PERFORMANCE: surfaced 13 knots; submerged 7 knots

U

U3

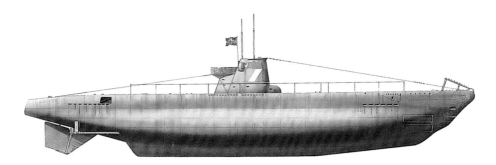

As early as 1922, the Germans set up a submarine design office at Den Haag (The Hague) in the Netherlands under cover of a Dutch firm. It was under the guise of constructing submarines for foreign navies that the German designers and constructors – who had remained in close touch since the end of World War I – set about producing craft which would actually serve as prototypes for a reborn German Navy. The last of five boats for Finland, the *Vessiko*, was built by the German firm Chrichton-Vulcan AB at Turku on the southwestern tip of Finland and given the designation Submarine *707*, although she was actually the prototype for the Type IIA U-boat. *U3* was a Type IIA. Because of her limited range, she was used mainly for training. She was paid off at Gdynia in July 1944 and cannibalized for spare parts early in 1945.

SPECIFICATIONS

COUNTRY: Germany
LAUNCH DATE: 1936
CREW: 25
DISPLACEMENT: surfaced 254 tonnes (250 tons); submerged 302 tonnes (298 tons)
DIMENSIONS: 40.9m x 4.1m x 3.8m (133ft 2in x 13ft 5in x 12ft 6in)
ARMAMENT: three 533mm (21in) torpedo tubes, one 20mm (0.8in) AA gun
POWERPLANT: twin screws, diesel/electric motors
RANGE: 1688km (912nm) at 10 knots
PERFORMANCE: surfaced 13 knots; submerged 7 knots

U21

The *U21* was one of a class of four U-boats, built at Danzig and completed in 1913. Although the Germans got away to a slow start in their submarine construction programme before World War I, the vessels were well engineered and used double hulls and twin screws from the start. German engineers refused to employ petrol engines in the early boats, preferring to use smellier but safer kerosene fuel. In 1908, suitable diesel engines were designed, and these were installed in the U19 class (to which *U21* belonged) and used exclusively thereafter. Of the four boats in the class, *U19* and *U22* surrendered in November 1918 and were scrapped at Blyth, Northumberland; *U20* was scuttled after being stranded on the Danish coast in 1916, and broken up in 1925; and *U21* foundered in the North Sea on 22 February 1919 as she was sailing to surrender.

SPECIFICATIONS

COUNTRY: Germany
LAUNCH DATE: 8 February 1913
CREW: 35
DISPLACEMENT: surfaced 660 tonnes (650 tons); submerged 850 tonnes (837 tons)
DIMENSIONS: 64.2m x 6.1m x 3.5m (210ft 6in x 20ft x 11ft 9in)
ARMAMENT: four 508mm (20in) torpedo tubes; one 86mm (3.4in) gun
POWERPLANT: two shafts, diesel/electric motors
RANGE: 9265km (5500nm) at 10 knots
PERFORMANCE: surfaced 15.4 knots; submerged 9.5 knots

U32

In September 1939, the German Navy had only 56 submarines in commission, and of these only 22 were ocean-going craft, suitable for service in the Atlantic. They were Type VIIs, the class to which *U32* belonged. With a conning tower only 5.2m (17ft) above the waterline they were hard to detect even in daylight, and under night conditions they were practically invisible. They could dive in less than half a minute; they could reach a depth of 100m (328ft) without strain and 200m (656ft) if hard pressed. They could maintain a submerged speed of 7.6 knots for two hours, or two knots for 130 hours. In fact, their depth and endurance performance at high speed was twice as good as that of any other submarine. *U32* was sunk in the North Atlantic on 30 October 1940 by the RN destroyers *Harvester* and *Highlander*.

SPECIFICATIONS
COUNTRY: Germany
LAUNCH DATE: 1937
CREW: 44
DISPLACEMENT: surfaced 636 tonnes (626 tons); submerged 757 tonnes (745 tons)
DIMENSIONS: 64.5m x 5.8m x 4.4m (211ft 6in x 19ft 3in x 14ft 6in)
ARMAMENT: five 533mm (21in) torpedo tubes; one 88mm (3.5in) gun; one 20mm AA gun
POWERPLANT: two screws, diesel/electric motors
RANGE: 6916km (3732nm) at 12 knots
PERFORMANCE: surfaced 16 knots; submerged 8 knots

U47

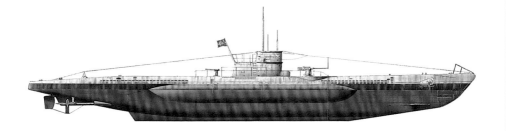

The Type VIIB U-boat was a slightly enlarged version of the Type VIIA, with a greater range and slightly higher surface speed. The most famous boat of this class was undoubtedly the *U47*, commanded by Lt Cdr Gunther Prien, who on the night of 13–14 October 1939 penetrated the defences of Scapa Flow and sank the 27,940-tonne (27,500-ton) battleship *Royal Oak*, a veteran of World War I, with three torpedo hits. The attack, in which 833 lives were lost, was carried out with great coolness, skill and daring, and came as a great shock to Britain. Prien returned home to a hero's welcome. He had already sunk three small merchant ships on the first day of the war, and went on to sink 27 more before *U47* was sunk in the North Atlantic on 7 March 1941 by the RN corvettes *Arbutus* and *Carmellia*.

SPECIFICATIONS

COUNTRY: Germany
LAUNCH DATE: 1938
CREW: 44
DISPLACEMENT: surfaced 765 tonnes (753 tons); submerged 871 tonnes (857 tons)
DIMENSIONS: 66.5m x 6.2m x 4.7m (218ft 2in x 20ft 3in x 15ft 6in)
ARMAMENT: five 533mm (21in) torpedo tubes; one 88mm (3.5in) gun; one 20mm AA gun
POWERPLANT: two-shaft diesel/electric motors
RANGE: 10,454km (5642nm) at 12 knots
PERFORMANCE: surfaced 17.2 knots; submerged 8 knots

U106

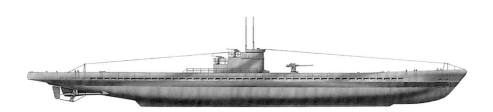

The Type IXB U-boats, of which *U106* was one, were improvements of the ocean-going Type IXAs with increased radius. Some Type IXBs were modified for service in the Far East, their range being increased to 16,100km (8700nm) at 12 knots. Their hunting ground was the Indian Ocean, using bases in Japanese-occupied Malaya and Singapore for replenishment. In March 1941, the *U106* (under Lt Cdr Oesten), having already sunk several merchant ships on her Atlantic patrols, torpedoed the British battleship *Malaya*, which was escorting a convoy. The battleship was repaired in New York, but was effectively out of the war. Under Capt Rasch, *U106* went on to sink many more merchantmen in the Atlantic before being destroyed by air attack off Cape Ortegal, Biscay, on 2 August 1943. Their high surface speed made the Type IXs very effective in surface night attacks.

SPECIFICATIONS

COUNTRY: Germany
LAUNCH DATE: 1939
CREW: 48
DISPLACEMENT: surfaced 1068 tonnes (1051 tons); submerged 2183 tonnes (1178 tons)
DIMENSIONS: 76.5m x 6.8m x 4.6m (251ft x 22ft 3in x 15ft 1in)
ARMAMENT: six 533mm (21in) torpedo tubes; one 102mm (4.1in) gun, one 20mm AA gun
POWERPLANT: twin shafts, diesel/electric motors
RANGE: 13,993km (7552nm) at 10 knots
PERFORMANCE: surfaced 18.2 knots; submerged 7.2 knots

U112

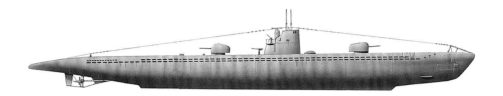

During World War I, as their primary aim was to sink merchant ships, German submarines were fitted with progressively heavier armament until eventually, boats of new construction carried two 150mm (5.9in) guns and older boats were modified to bring them up to a similar standard. These weapons could outrange any gun mounted for defensive purposes in merchant vessels, so that U-boats could destroy their victims by gunfire in surface actions, reserving their torpedoes for more dangerous, high-value warship targets. A special class of long-range boat, the submarine cruiser, was designed, and in World War II this concept was resurrected in the Type XI class of U-boat. Designated *U112* to *U115*, the boats were to have carried a spotter aircraft to extend their radius of observation. However, the class never got beyond the project stage.

SPECIFICATIONS

COUNTRY: Germany
LAUNCH DATE: projected only
CREW: 110
DISPLACEMENT: surfaced 3190 tonnes (3140 tons); submerged 3688 tonnes (3630 tons)
DIMENSIONS: 115m x 9.5m x 6m (377ft 4in x 31ft 2in x 19ft 8in)
ARMAMENT: eight 533mm (21in) torpedo tubes; four 127mm (5in) guns; two 30mm (1.18in) and two 20mm (0.79in) AA guns
POWERPLANT: two shafts, diesel/electric motors
RANGE: 25,266km (13,635nm) at 12 knots
PERFORMANCE: surfaced 23 knots; submerged 7 knots

U139

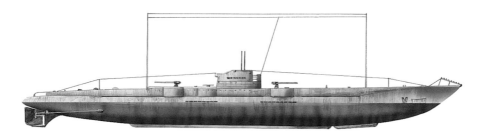

In 1917 the Germans converted two U151 class submarines – *U151* and *U155* – as long-range cargo-carrying vessels. One, the *Deutschland*, made two commercial runs to the United States before America's entry into the war brought an end to the venture; being converted back to naval use along with her sister vessel, *Oldenburg*. The boats were reclassified as submarine cruisers and more were laid down, including *U139*, *U140* and *U141*. The first two were among the very few German submarines to be given names, probably because of their intended role as surface combatants for the most part; the *U139* became the *Kapitanleutnant Schweiger*, and the *U140* *Kapitanleutnant Weddingen*. After the war *U139* was allocated to France as the Halbronn, *U140* was sunk as a gunnery target by an American destroyer, and *U141* was scrapped in 1923.

SPECIFICATIONS

COUNTRY: Germany
LAUNCH DATE: 3 December 1917
CREW: 62
DISPLACEMENT: surfaced 1961 tonnes (1930 tons); submerged 2523 tonnes (2483 tons)
DIMENSIONS: 94.8m x 9m x 5.2m (311ft x 29ft 9in x 17ft 3in)
ARMAMENT: six 508mm (20in) torpedo tubes; two 150mm (5.9in) guns
POWERPLANT: twin shafts, diesel/electric motors
RANGE: 23,390km (12,630nm) at 8 knots
PERFORMANCE: surfaced 15.8 knots; submerged 7.6 knots

U140

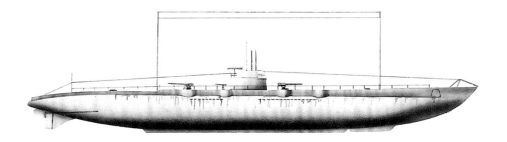

The *U140* mentioned in the previous entry, was one of three 'submarine cruisers' of the *U139* class, two of which were named. The Germans also took the unusual step of allocating names to the boats of two succeeding classes, *U145* to *U147* and *U148* to *U150*. These boats, also classed as submarine cruisers, were named *Kapitanleutnant Wegener* (*U145*), *Oberleutnant-zur-Zee Saltzwedel* (*U146*), *Kapitanleutnant Hansen* (*U147*), *Oberleutnant-zur-Zee Pustkuchen* (*U148*), *Kapitanleutnant Freiherr von Berkheim* (*U149*) and *Kapitanleutnant Schneider* (*U150*). The first three boats were laid down at the A.G. Vulcan yard, Hamburg, the others at A.G. Weser, Bremen. All six boats were broken up before completion; *U145* to *U147* were actually launched in June – September 1918, but by then the war was nearly over.

SPECIFICATIONS

COUNTRY: Germany
LAUNCH DATE: 04 November 1917
CREW: 62
DISPLACEMENT: surfaced 1961 tonnes (1930 tons); submerged 2523 tonnes (2483 tons)
DIMENSIONS: 94.8m x 9m x 5.2m (311ft x 29ft 9in x 17ft 3in)
ARMAMENT: six 508mm (20in) torpedo tubes; two 150mm (5.9in) guns
POWERPLANT: twin shafts, diesel/electric motors
RANGE: 32,873km (17,750nm) at 8 knots
PERFORMANCE: surfaced 15.8 knots; submerged 7.6 knots

U151

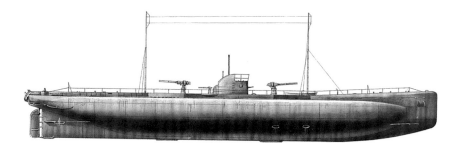

Before America's entry into the war in 1917 the Germans were quick to recognize the potential of large, cargo-carrying submarines as a means of beating the blockade imposed on Germany's ports by the Royal Navy. Two U151-class submarines, the *U151* and *U155*, were converted for mercantile use and named *Oldenburg* and *Deutschland* respectively. After America's entry into the war, the two boats were converted back to naval use as heavily-armed submarine cruisers, forming two of a class of seven (*U151* to *U157*). On 24 November 1918, *U151* was surrendered to France and was sunk as a target vessel off Cherbourg on 7 June 1921. *U155*, formerly *Deutschland*, was scrapped at Morecambe, England, in 1922, while a third merchant conversion, *Bremen*, was lost on her first voyage in 1917, possibly mined off the Orkneys.

SPECIFICATIONS

COUNTRY: Germany
LAUNCH DATE: 04 April 1917
CREW: 56
DISPLACEMENT: surfaced 1536 tonnes (1512 tons); submerged 1905 tonnes (1875 tons)
DIMENSIONS: 65m x 8.9m x 5.3m (213ft 3in x 29ft 2in x 17ft 5in)
ARMAMENT: two 509mm (20in) torpedo tubes; two 150mm (5.9in) and two 86mm (3.4in) guns
POWERPLANT: twin-screw diesel engines, electric motors
RANGE: 20,909km (11,284nm) at 10 knots
PERFORMANCE: surfaced 12.4 knots; submerged 5.2 knots

U160

The *U160* was leader of a class of 13 fast U-boats laid down in the last months of the war. She was built by Bremer Vulcan at Kiel. Five of these boats, *U168* to *U172*, were scrapped before they were completed. Of the remainder, *U160* was surrendered to France and scrapped at Cherbourg in 1922; *U161* was stranded en route to the breakers; *U162* was also surrendered to the French, serving as the Pierre Marast before being scrapped in 1937; *U163* was handed over to Italy and scrapped in 1919; *U164* was scrapped at Swansea in 1922; *U165* was sunk by accident in the Weser; *U166* was completed after the Armistice and handed over to France, serving as the Jean Roulier before going to the breaker's yard in 1935; and *U167* was scrapped in 1921. Because of their high speed, boats of this class usually attacked on the surface.

SPECIFICATIONS

COUNTRY: Germany
LAUNCH DATE: 27 February 1918
CREW: 39
DISPLACEMENT: surfaced 834 tonnes (821 tons); submerged 1016 tonnes (1000 tons)
DIMENSIONS: 71.8m x 6.2m x 4.1m (235ft 6in x 20ft 6in x 13ft 6in)
ARMAMENT: six 509mm (20in) torpedo tubes; two 104mm (4.1in) guns
POWERPLANT: two shafts, diesel/electric motors
RANGE: 15,372km (8300nm) at 8 knots
PERFORMANCE: surfaced 16.2 knots; submerged 8.2 knots

UB4

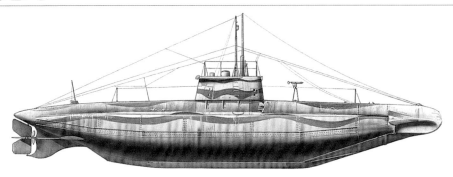

In 1914, the Germans began construction of a new series of U-boats, the small UB coastal class. Upon completion, the majority of these were sent by rail in sections to Antwerp in Belgium, which was in German hands, or Pola, the Austro-Hungarian port on the Adriatic, where they were assembled and made ready for deployment. There were no fewer than 25 classes of UB boats, the designs growing rapidly larger as the war progressed. There were eight boats in UB4's class, of which *UB1* was wrecked in the Adriatic and scrapped, *UB2* was stricken in 1919, *UB3* was missing in the Aegean Sea, *UB4* was sunk in the North Sea by the RN armed trawler *Inverlyon* in August 1915, *UB5* was stricken in 1919, *UB6* was surrendered to France, *UB7* was sunk in the Black Sea and *UB8* was handed over to France.

SPECIFICATIONS

COUNTRY: Germany
LAUNCH DATE: April 1915
CREW: 14
DISPLACEMENT: surfaced 129 tonnes (127 tons); submerged 144 tonnes (142 tons)
DIMENSIONS: 28m x 2.9m x 3m (92ft 3in x 9ft 9in x 10ft)
ARMAMENT: two 457mm (18in) torpedo tubes
POWERPLANT: single screw, diesel/electric motors
RANGE: 2778km (1599nm) at 5 knots
PERFORMANCE: surfaced 6.5 knots; submerged 5.5 knots

UC74

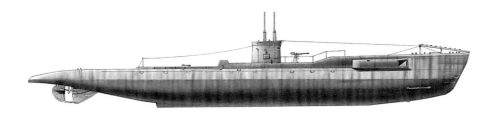

U C74 was one of a class of six
minelaying submarines, all launched
in October to December 1917 and built by
A.G. Vulcan, Hamburg. The boats were fitted
with six vertical mine tubes. UC74 served
briefly with the Austrian Navy as the U93,
but with a German crew. At the end of World
War I, she was interned at Barcelona, having
been forced to put in there through lack
of fuel, and was surrendered to France in
1919. She was scrapped at Toulon in 1921.
Of the other boats, UC75 was sunk in the
North Sea by the destroyer HMS Fairy;
UC76 was accidentally lost off Heligoland
when her mines exploded, salvaged and
recommissioned, and eventually interned at
Karlskrona, Sweden; UC77 and UC78 were
sunk by RN drifters in the Dover Straits,
while UC79 was mined and sunk in the
same area.

SPECIFICATIONS

COUNTRY: Germany
LAUNCH DATE: 19 October 1916
CREW: 26
DISPLACEMENT: surfaced 416 tonnes (410 tons);
submerged 500 tonnes (492 tons)
DIMENSIONS: 50.6m x 5.1m x 3.6m (166ft x 16ft 9in
x 12ft)
ARMAMENT: three 508mm (20in) torpedo tubes, one
86mm (3.4in) gun, 18 mines
POWERPLANT: two-shaft diesel/electric motors
RANGE: 18,520km (10,000nm) at 10 knots
PERFORMANCE: surfaced 11.8 knots; submerged 7.3
knots

Uebi Scebeli

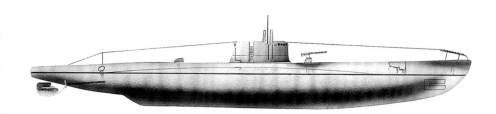

Uebi Scebeli was one of the Adua class of 17 short-range vessels, only one of which, *Alagi*, was destined to survive World War II. *Uebi Scebeli* herself was an early casualty; on 29 June 1940 she was attacked by British destroyers and depth-charged to the surface, coming under fire from five of the warships. She was scuttled by her crew. The Adua class were among the best Italian submarines to be used during the war, giving good service in a variety of roles; although their surface speed was low they were strong and very manoeuvrable. The early boats of the class took part in the Spanish Civil War and all except one (the *Macalle*, which was in the Red Sea) operated in the Mediterranean. Two of the Aduas were modified in 1940–41 for the carriage of human torpedoes. These boats might well be described as the most versatile in Italian service.

SPECIFICATIONS

COUNTRY: Italy
LAUNCH DATE: 12 January 1937
CREW: 45
DISPLACEMENT: surfaced 691 tonnes (680 tons); submerged 880 tonnes (866 tons)
DIMENSIONS: 60.2m x 6.5m x 4.6m (197ft 6in x 21ft 4in x 15ft 1in)
ARMAMENT: six 530mm (21in) torpedo tubes, one 100mm (4in) gun
POWERPLANT: two diesel engines, two electric motors
RANGE: 9260km (5000nm) at 8 knots
PERFORMANCE: surfaced 14 knots; submerged 7 knots

Velella

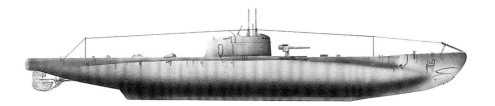

In 1931, Portugal ordered two submarines from the CRDA Yards, but later cancelled them for economic reasons, so they were completed for the Italian Navy under the names *Argo* and *Velella*. This accounted for the lengthy delay between the boats being laid down in October 1931 and their respective launch dates of November and December 1936; *Argo* was completed on 31 August 1937 and *Velella* the next day. *Velella* saw much war service, sinking at least two merchant vessels, before being sunk herself by HMS *Shakespeare* (under Lt Ainslie) in the Gulf of Salerno. Her sister vessel *Argo* was scuttled in the Monfalcone CRDA yards on 11 September 1943 to avoid being captured by the Germans after the Armistice. The Germans were denied the use of many potentially valuable warships in this way.

SPECIFICATIONS

COUNTRY: Italy
LAUNCH DATE: 12 December 1936
CREW: 46
DISPLACEMENT: surfaced 807 tonnes (794 tons); submerged 1034 tonnes (1018 tons)
DIMENSIONS: 63m x 6.9m x 4.5m (206ff 8in x 22ft 9in x 14ft 8in)
ARMAMENT: six 533mm (21in) torpedo tubes; one 100mm (3.9in) gun
POWERPLANT: twin screws, diesel/electric motors
RANGE: 9260km (5000nm) at 8 knots
PERFORMANCE: surfaced 14 knots; submerged 8 knots

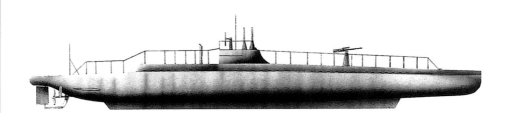

Following a fact-finding visit to Fiat-San Giorgio in 1911, a British Admiralty team next went to the Schneider Yard at Toulon to study submarine designs using the then revolutionary and advanced double-hull method of submarine construction, and also drop collars for torpedoes, enabling the weapons to be attached externally. As a result of these investigations, the Admiralty placed an order with Armstrong-Whitworth for four new boats using these innovations, known as the W class, the first two being laid down in 1913. However, by 1916, the Royal Navy had a surplus of non-standard medium-sized submarines, and so it was decided to hand *W1* and *W2* over to the Italian Navy. They had poor manoeuvrability and often suffered diesel breakdowns. Both saw limited war service, and were used mainly for training. *W2* was stricken in 1919.

SPECIFICATIONS

COUNTRY: Italy
LAUNCH DATE: February 1915
CREW: 19
DISPLACEMENT: surfaced 336 tonnes (331 tons); submerged 507 tonnes (499 tons)
DIMENSIONS: 52.4m x 4.7m x 2.7m (172ft x 15ft 5in x 8ft 10in)
ARMAMENT: two 457mm (18in) torpedo tubes
POWERPLANT: twin screws, diesel/electric motors
RANGE: 4630km (2500nm) at 9 knots
PERFORMANCE: surfaced 13 knots; submerged 8.5 knots

Walrus

Walrus was one of an eight-unit class developed from earlier American submarines. Trouble was experienced at first with her NLSE diesel engines, and in spite of these being throroughly stripped and overhauled, the problem was never completely cured in three of the class. The diesel engines developed 708kW (950hp) and the electric motors 507kW (680hp). Diving depth was 61m (200ft). *Walrus*, the last US submarine to be given a name for many years to come, was later renumbered *K4*. She served in the Azores during World War I, and was broken up in 1931. Many of the American submarine classes built during the World War I period were designed for purely defensive use, and were not really suitable for oceanic operations. Nevertheless, many were still on the active list when American entered the next war.

SPECIFICATIONS

COUNTRY: United States
LAUNCH DATE: March 1914
CREW: 31
DISPLACEMENT: surfaced 398 tonnes (392 tons); submerged 530 tonnes (521 tons)
DIMENSIONS: 47m x 5m x 4m (153ft 10in x 16ft 9in x 13ft 2in)
ARMAMENT: four 457mm (18in) torpedo tubes
POWERPLANT: twin screws, diesel/electric motors
RANGE: 8334km (4500nm) at 10 knots
PERFORMANCE: surfaced 14 knots; submerged 10.5 knots

X1

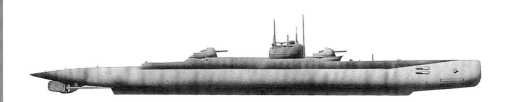

X1 was designed to evaluate the performance of a very large submarine underwater; she would probably never have existed at all had it not been for the legacy of the large German 'submarine cruisers' of World War I, which, although few became operational, left behind an inflated reputation. They seemed to validate the concept of a big submersible carrying a heavy armament, which could fight it out on the surface with destroyers and armed merchant cruisers. *X1*, unlike other prototype craft of her type, proved to have excellent handling qualities and was a steady gun platform; she was also one of the first submarines to have ASDIC detection equipment. She was the only Royal Navy vessel laid down after World War I to be scrapped before the start of the second conflict, being broken up in 1936.

SPECIFICATIONS

COUNTRY: United Kingdom
LAUNCH DATE: 1925
CREW: 75
DISPLACEMENT: surfaced 3098 tonnes (3050 tons); submerged 3657 tonnes (3600 tons)
DIMENSIONS: 110.8m x 9m x 4.8m (363ft 6in x 29ft 10in x 15ft 9in)
ARMAMENT: six 533mm (21in) torpedo tubes; four 132mm (5.2in) guns
POWERPLANT: twin screws, diesel/electric motors
RANGE: not known
PERFORMANCE: surfaced 20 knots; submerged 9 knots

X2 (1917)

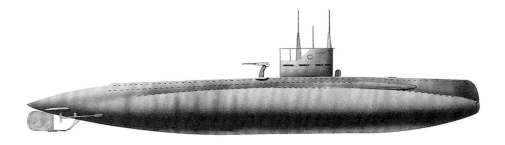

X2 was a single-hulled minelaying submarine with 'saddle' tanks, based on the Austrian *U24* (ex-German *UC12*) which sank off Taranto after hitting one of her own mines. She was later raised by the Italians, who commissioned her as the *X1* and scrapped her in May 1919. *X2* was laid down on 22 August 1916 and completed on 1 February 1918. She could dive to a maximum depth of 40m (130ft); her submerged range at 3 knots was 112km (60nm). A third boat in this minelayer class was also built and designated *X3*; she was launched on 29 December 1917 and completed on 27 August 1918. Both ships had nine tubes for a total capacity of 18 mines. The boats were slow and had poor manoeuvrability. They were laid up on 16 September 1940. In both world wars, minelaying was a key activity of the Italian Navy.

SPECIFICATIONS

COUNTRY: Italy
LAUNCH DATE: 25 April 1917
CREW: 14
DISPLACEMENT: surfaced 409 tonnes (403 tons); submerged 475 tonnes (468 tons)
DIMENSIONS: 42.6m x 5.5m x 3m (139ft 9in x 18ft x 10ft 4in)
ARMAMENT: two 450mm (17.7in) torpedo tubes; one 76mm (3in) gun
POWERPLANT: twin screws, diesel/electric motors
RANGE: 2280km (1229nm) at 16 knots
PERFORMANCE: surfaced 8.2 knots; submerged 6.2 knots

X2 (1934)

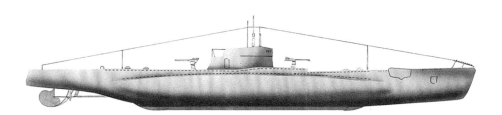

The *X2* was formerly the Italian Archimede class submarine *Galileo Galilei*. When Italy entered World War II, she was based in the Red Sea and, on 19 October 1940, she was captured after a fierce battle with the British armed trawler *Moonstone* during which nearly all her officers were killed and the remaining crew – still inside the boat – were poisoned by emissions from the air conditioning system. In British service, the *X2* carried the pennant number *P711*; she served in the East Indies from 1941 to 1944 as a training boat before returning to the Mediterrranean in 1944. She was scrapped in 1946. Two other Italian boats captured on active service, the *Perla* and *Tosi* (*P712* and *P714*) were also used in the training role, the former serving in the Royal Hellenic Navy as the Matrozos.

SPECIFICATIONS

COUNTRY: Britain
LAUNCH DATE: 19 March 1934
CREW: 49
DISPLACEMENT: surfaced 1000 tonnes (985 tons); submerged 1280 tonnes (1259 tons)
DIMENSIONS: 70.5m x 6.8m x 4m (231ft 3in x 22ft 4in x 13ft 6in)
ARMAMENT: eight 533mm (21in) torpedo tubes; two 100mm (3.9in) guns
POWERPLANT: twin screws, diesel/electric motors
RANGE: 6270km (3379nm) at 16 knots
PERFORMANCE: surfaced 17 knots; submerged 8.5 knots

Zoea

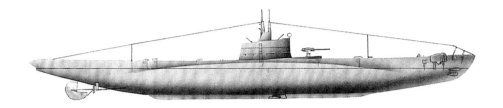

Zoea was one of three minelaying submarines built for the Italian Navy just before World War II, the others being *Atropo* and *Foca*. As first completed, their 100mm (3.9in) gun was mounted in a training turret, in the after part of the conning tower. This gun was later removed and mounted in the traditional deck position, forward of the conning tower. The class leader, *Foca*, was lost on 15 October 1940 while laying a mine barrage off Haifa, Palestine; it was thought that she had probably run into a British minefield. *Atropo* and *Zoea* survived the war and were discarded in 1947. In common with many other Italian submarines, they were in very poor condition by this time. Late in 1943, *Zoea* was used by the Allies to run supplies to British garrisons on the Aegean islands of Samos and Leros.

SPECIFICATIONS

COUNTRY: Italy
LAUNCH DATE: 3 February 1936
CREW: 60
DISPLACEMENT: surfaced 1354 tonnes (1333 tons); submerged 1685 tonnes (1659 tons)
DIMENSIONS: 82.8m x 7.2m x 5.3m (271ft 8in x 23ft 6in x 17ft 5in)
ARMAMENT: six 533mm (21in) torpedo tubes; one 100mm (3.9in) gun
POWERPLANT: twin-screw diesel engines, electric motors
RANGE: 15,742km (8500nm) at 8 knots
PERFORMANCE: surfaced 15.2 knots; submerged 7.4 knots

Index

WEAPONS OF WAR